WOMEN AND THE WORLD ECONOMIC CRISIS

WOMEN AND WORLD DEVELOPMENT SERIES

This series has been developed by the UN/NGO Group on Women and Development and makes available the most recent information, debate and action being taken on world development issues, and the impact on women. Each volume is fully illustrated and attractively presented. Each outlines its particular subject, as well as including an introduction to resources and guidance on how to use the books in workshops and seminars. The aim of each title is to bring women's concerns more directly and effectively into the development process, and to achieve an improvement in women's status in our rapidly changing world.

The Group was established in 1980 to organise the production and distribution of joint UN/NGO development education materials. It was the first time that United Nations agencies and non-governmental organisations had collaborated in this way, and the Group remains a unique example of cooperation between international and non-governmental institutions. Membership of the Programme Group is open to all interested organisations.

SERIES TITLES – in order of scheduled publication: 1991–92

● **WOMEN AND THE WORLD ECONOMIC CRISIS**
PREPARED BY JEANNE VICKERS / WINTER 1990 / 91

● **WOMEN AND DISABILITY**
PREPARED BY ESTHER R. BOYLAN / SPRING 1991

● **WOMEN AND THE ENVIRONMENT**
PREPARED BY ANNABEL RODDA / SUMMER 1991

● **WOMEN AND HEALTH**
PREPARED BY PATRICIA SMYKE / AUTUMN 1991

● **REFUGEE WOMEN**
PREPARED BY SUSAN FORBES MARTIN / WINTER 1991 / 92

● **WOMEN AND LITERACY**
PREPARED BY MARCELA BALLARA / SPRING 1992

● **WOMEN AND THE FAMILY**
AUTUMN 1992

● **WOMEN AT WORK**
WINTER 1992 / 93

For full details, as well as order forms, please write to:
ZED BOOKS LTD, 57 CALEDONIAN ROAD, LONDON N1 9BU, U.K.

WOMEN AND THE WORLD ECONOMIC CRISIS

PREPARED BY JEANNE VICKERS

Zed Books Ltd · London & New Jersey

Women and the World Economic Crisis was first published by Zed Books Ltd,
57 Caledonian Road, London N1 9BU, United Kingdom and 171 First Avenue,
Atlantic Highlands, New Jersey 07716, United States of America, in 1991.

Copyright © United Nations Non-Governmental Liaison Service, 1991

Cover and book design by Lee Robinson
Cover photo: P. Jaxa
Typeset by Goodfellow & Egan, Cambridge
Printed and bound in the United Kingdom at The Bath Press, Avon

British Library Cataloguing in Publication Data

Women and the World Economic Crisis. – (Women and World Development).
1. Developing countries. Economic conditions. Role of women
I. Vickers, Jeanne   II. Series
330.91724
ISBN 0-86232-974-4
ISBN 0-86232-975-2 pbk

Library of Congress Cataloging-in-Publication Data

Vickers, Jeanne.
    Women and the world economic crisis/prepared by Jeanne Vickers.
        p.   cm. – (Women and world development series)
    ISBN 0–86232–974–4 (cloth). – ISBN 0–86232–975–2 (paper)
    1. Women – Developing countries. – Economic conditions. 2. Women in
development – Developing countries. 3. Developing countries – Economic
conditions. 4. International economic relations.
I. Title. II. Series.
HO1870.9.V53   1991
305.42'09172'4 – dc20
                                                                90–28525
                                                                CIP

CONTENTS

ACKNOWLEDGEMENTS

This book has been prepared by Jeanne Vickers on behalf of the Joint UN-NGO Group on Women and Development, and made possible through financial contributions from:

- United Nations Division for the Advancement of Women (DAW)
- United Nations Children's Fund (UNICEF)
- United Nations High Commissioner for Refugees (UNHCR)
- The Official Aid Agency of Finland (FINNIDA)
- Ministry of Foreign Affairs, Denmark (DANIDA)

The content of this book has been approved by the Joint UN-NGO Group on Women and Development. The following organisations have made a special contribution through their participation in the editorial panel formed for this publication:

- United Nations Children's Fund (UNICEF)
- International Labour Office (ILO)
- World Federation of Methodist Women
- International Council of Jewish Women
- Women's International League for Peace and Freedom
- International Council of Social Welfare
- Zonta International

EDITOR'S NOTE

WOMEN AND THE WORLD ECONOMIC CRISIS has been written to illustrate the links between the various factors which have given rise to the world economic crisis; to show the effects of that crisis, and of adjustment policies, upon vulnerable groups – especially women; and to examine the ways in which people and groups have responded by creating their own opportunities for survival and development. It has been compiled from a variety of sources so as to provide a global perspective and a wide spectrum of cultural perspectives on the themes and issues concerned.

It is important to note that it is strictly focussed on debt and adjustment issues and their effect upon development in general and upon women in particular. Chapters 1 and 2 analyse in depth the origins and mechanisms of the world economic crisis, including the impact of the international debt problem and of structural adjustment policies as distinct from the severe 'ordinary' consequences of under-development. Chapters 3, 4 and 5 detail policy responses on the part of governments and intergovernmental bodies, non-governmental organisations, and action groups at the grassroots level. Chapters 6 to 10 contain case studies on five developing countries which have been severely affected by the crisis. Chapter 11 deals with the concepts of solidarity and of co-responsibility for the economic crisis.

Annex I gives a glossary of the terms to be found every day in our newspapers in relation to the subject, while Annex II provides materials and guidance for group or individual study and action on a subject about which all too little is known. Annex III contains a list of organisations active in questions relating to debt, adjustment and women, followed by a selective bibliography. The book's main thrust is that there is a great need to enlighten public opinion and attitudes with regard to the role of women at a time of extreme economic and social upheaval, in both industrialised and developing countries, and of accelerating global interdependence.

JEANNE VICKERS

INTRODUCTION

BY DR. KRISHNA AHOOJA-PATEL[1]

IT IS IMPORTANT, when dealing with a subject as complicated as the world economic crisis and its relationship to women, to be extremely clear about our understanding of the term. How do we define 'the world economic crisis', its effects in developing Third World countries and in those of the North, its causes and consequences to the ordinary human being, and especially to women?

Put simply, the world economic crisis has been caused by a multiplicity of inter-related factors which have led to a global slowdown in both economic activity and development. First, in an attempt to recycle the US dollar surpluses caused by the huge rise in oil prices in the early 1970s, Western banks offered 'cheap money' to developing countries and encouraged them to take large loans for development purposes at what were then reasonable interest rates. Given the high price of oil, Mexico, for instance, borrowed heavily in order to increase its oil production capacity, so that a few years later, when oil prices fell but interest rates soared to as high as 18–20%, the country found itself in a very difficult debt situation.

Then a new rise in oil prices in 1978-79 precipitated a major world recession; industrialised countries' growth rates fell rapidly and this in turn depressed markets in the Third World, which could not sell its products. Commodity prices fell precipitately; developing countries had to pay higher prices for imports while receiving lower prices for exports. The rise in protectionism in the industrialised countries made access to their markets even more difficult. The Third World could neither earn nor borrow what it needed; development aid stagnated and private lending simply disappeared.

Last but not least, world military expenditures in 1986 (the International Year of Peace) reached an all-time high of $900 billion, and have now passed the $1,000 billion mark. The Swedish International Peace Research Institute (SIPRI) has proposed ways in which funds released through disarmament can be used for development purposes, particularly with regard to conversion from defence to civil industries, and suggests that there is 'an automatic link between ... military expenditure and the global economic crisis'.[2] (According to Ruth Leger Sivard, arms imports of developing countries have been a major cause of the world economic crisis. During the period 1975-85 they accounted for 40% of the increase in the foreign debt of developing countries. The military expenditures of these countries have increased six-fold since 1960, unemployment eight-fold.[3]

Women are wage earners or small-scale entrepreneurs; they are mothers, home-workers, migrants and of course they are also citizens of a state. There are also women refugees and stateless women. They have multiple roles and are not a homogeneous group. In which role are they affected most by these crises under whose shadow we all live? When women as part of a heterogeneous group look at the economic crisis, what do they perceive? And how does what they see influence their lives? What are the alternative approaches to the development crisis at the national level? Do these approaches relate to women? What is the impact on women of the inter-relationship between national and international policies?

WOMEN'S ROLE IN DEVELOPMENT PLANS

☐ The world economic crisis influences the daily life of women everywhere, and in turn has been influenced by the fact that, in the 1970s, the central debate on development planning did not consider women as part of the complexity called 'economic structures'. At no stage of formulation or implementation of national development plans were they or their interests present, and in no development plan as yet have women achieved equality in allocation of resources or investment targets.

The earlier preoccupations of development practitioners of the 1970s with the new international economic order (NIEO, 1974), the basic needs strategies (1976) and policies of collective self-reliance (1979), have given way more recently to structural adjustment policies and programmes. These were considered by some to be the panacea to balance the consequences of development deficiencies. Although in the 1980s the needs and interests of women began to be partially recognised, out of 96 countries recently surveyed by the UN International Research and Training Institute for the Advancement of Women (INSTRAW), in only six countries were women's issues accorded a place in the text of the development plan.

From available research, surveys and reports within and outside the UN system written by economists, social scientists and 'Women in Development' specialists under the title 'World Economic Crisis', one common feature stands out: the poor have been hurt the most by the crisis and by structural adjustment programmes. Women have been particularly affected because many of the poor are women, and because women were already faced with socio-economic bias, which made them even more vulnerable.

For example, migrant and refugee women are more vulnerable than migrant and refugee men; women as industrial workers receive lower wages than men;

women who regularly perform agricultural tasks are not accounted for or even given the status of workers; and women as citizens are less able than men to exercise their economic and social rights. The 1988 UN World Economic Survey (Selected Indicators of the Socio-economic Attainment of Women) even notes that 'published data give the impression that in developing countries the majority of women play *no role in the economy*' (emphasis added).

Women are, indeed, directly and indirectly linked to the world economy[4] – and to the world economic crisis – by visible and invisible threads. Understanding the crisis from women's point of view signifies that one of the underlying reasons for its continuation and perpetuation is that women are excluded from decision-making at the national and international levels. There is a strong indication that several aspects of the economic crisis could be overcome if women were an integral part of the solution.

Policy changes Several UN agencies have been giving increasing attention to this aspect. The United Nations Division for the Advancement of Women organised an Interregional Seminar in Vienna from 3 to 7 October 1988 which raised some fundamental issues on the direct and indirect impact of the economic crisis on women, based on national and regional statistics. Chapter 2 of its 1989 Update of the Survey on the Role of Women in Development is devoted to the effects on women of international debt and adjustment policies and the stagnation in real growth in developing countries (especially in Africa). It also studies the ways in which women themselves are working towards a solution of problems caused both by the economic crisis and by structural adjustment policies.

There is a growing international consensus that indebtedness and structural adjustment policies must be determined with full consideration of their effects upon people. How this can be done with regard to women is a question of vital importance. It is crucial to analyse simultaneously the social, educational and political structures that have frequently been left out of the global analysis, but that have an immediate, and often devastating, impact upon women.

1   Dr Krishna Ahooja-Patel is former Deputy Director of the United Nations International Research and Training Institute for the Advancement of Women (INSTRAW). The views expressed in this article should not be attributed to the United Nations organisation of which she was a staff member.
2   Saadeg Deger, *SIPRI Yearbook 1988*, Stockholm.
3   Ruth Leger Sivard, *World Military and Social Expenditures 1986*. World Priorities, Box 25140, Washington DC 20007. See also 1987/88 edition.
4   INSTRAW/Susan Joekes, *Women in the World Economy*. United Nations International Research and Training Institute for the Advancement of Women. Oxford University Press, 1987.

ORIGINS & MECHANISMS OF THE CRISIS

In observing International Women's Day 1988 we must also look at the gender implications of the debt crisis that threatens many developing nations. During the process of structural adjustment, countries striving to reduce their debt are confronted with painful choices. Assistance is needed in the design of adjustment policies in order that the burden imposed be fairly distributed and that the bulk of the poorest – a large share of whom are women – do not suffer disproportionately.

JAVIER PÉREZ DE CUÉLLAR, UN SECRETARY-GENERAL
8 MARCH 1988

AT A UN/NGO WORKSHOP held in Oxford in September 1987 on the theme Debt, Adjustment and the Needs of the Poor, Frances Stewart (Senior Research Fellow, Queen Elizabeth House, Oxford) gave a very clear analysis of the conditions which have given rise to the world economic crisis. After decades of fairly steady progress during which mortality rates fell and life expectancy rose, she said, the 1980s saw a major tragic reversal in the human condition. Everyone needed to recognise the main cause of the reversal, which was not a sudden deterioration in the internal policies of developing countries but in the external conditions they faced, due to adverse changes in the world economy.[1]

In most parts of the world, the 1950s and 1960s, and to some extent the 1970s, had been a time of fairly steady progress in terms of economic growth and trade liberalisation. But in the early 1970s the rise in oil prices forced many countries to borrow heavily in order to meet the big additional costs which resulted; those who could switched to private borrowing and more or less managed to maintain economic growth. And at the end of the 1970s came a further series of shocks.

First, in 1978-79, was a new rise in oil prices, which precipitated a major world recession from which the industrialised countries have still not fully recovered; their growth rates were only half or two-thirds those of the 1970s, and this in turn depressed markets in the Third World. The second major shock was the unprecedented fall in commodity prices, which has still not been reversed. In 1988 alone, Africa lost something in the region of $19 billion. And the third shock was rising protectionism in the industrialised countries; Third World countries had to pay higher prices for imports while receiving lower prices for exports. The fall in their purchasing power meant that they could import much less than before. A World Bank study has concluded that the cost to developing countries of rich-country protectionism exceeds the value of international aid.[2]

Not only could they no longer earn what they needed, they could no longer borrow it either, for interest rates rose to enormous heights in the early 1980s – to 18-20%. In addition, private lending simply disappeared in the 1980s, and development aid stagnated. According to Ms Stewart, a net positive inflow of $38 billion to the capital account of developing countries in 1979 was transformed by 1986 into a net negative outflow of $50 billion – a huge deterioration. Hence the 'debt crisis'.[3]

But there was yet another shock, she said. Developing countries were forced to go to the only lender who would still lend to them: the International Monetary Fund (IMF), whose programmes called for

1

severe cutbacks in government expenditure, in employment, in credit creation and, wherever possible, in subsidies. As a result, the incomes of the poor were squeezed, prices rocketed, and basic health and education services were often reduced by the government.

Statistics show that real wages during the 1980s fell by 40% in Mexico; in Ghana they were just a quarter of the level of 1974. Unemployment was over 25% in Jamaica and during the 1980s it rose from 10% to 16% in Chile and from 5% to 11% in Peru. In Latin America the proportion of the labour force in the informal sector increased by some 10%, but here, too, incomes were depressed. Food prices rose steeply. In Ghana even households with two wage-earners had only enough money to purchase 30% of an adequate diet; government expenditure on education in 1982 was only 30% of what it had been in 1974 in real terms, and on health only 23%. In Jamaica there was a fall of 40% per head in social service expenditure in the 1980s.[4]

In 1989 the international community was increasingly concerned with the social effects of adjustment programmes, and the attention of governments and international institutions now focuses on the need to minimise the costs of adjustment to the poorer groups and to have adjustment with growth. It is important in this respect to study the specific effect of the crisis upon women.

THE RECESSION OF THE EIGHTIES □

Thus, between 1981 and 1986 the world economy, and particularly the developing market economies as a whole, experienced the most severe and prolonged recession since the 1930s. While most countries in South and East Asia managed to maintain reasonable rates of growth over the period, 70% of the countries in Africa, the Middle East and Latin America experienced negative cumulative growth rates in GDP per capita according to the UNICEF study *Adjustment with a Human Face*. Although the situation in OECD countries somewhat improved in 1984-86, the majority of developing nations outside Asia continued to be affected by the unfavourable world environment. In 1984-85, drought was a serious contributory factor, particularly in Africa, followed by devastating damage from floods in Bangladesh and hurricanes in the Caribbean.

But the depressed state of the world economy in the 1980s was due mainly to international economic factors. As Susan Joekes points out in her study for the UN's International Research and Training Institute for Women, greater international interdependence has undoubtedly contributed to world economic growth over the post-war period, but it also implies vulnerability, and events in the past two decades have shown not only the inherent fragility of certain aspects of the modern world economy but also the consequences of unequal international economic relations.

Prices of developing countries' imports and exports and the value of their currencies had fluctuated unpredictably in the 1970s, while countries had become more vulnerable to such instability with their participation in the expansion of international trade and payments since the Second World War. Countries whose terms of trade deteriorated had only one way out, and that was to take advantage (as it seemed then) of the rapidly increasing supplies of international money to promote continued investment. Then three things happened together: most developing countries' export earnings fell away; the cost of their imports rose; and the price of current and outstanding credit to bridge the gap rose.

Extreme indebtedness or drastic cutbacks in imports of consumer goods and industrial supplies were the only possible results; most countries suffered both. The instability of exchange rates led to massive speculation, followed by later outflows of capital, which intensified the need for external credit. International aid, which would have been some compensation, decreased in real terms even below promised levels... The real cost of these strains on the international financial markets fell on the people, particularly the poorest. Falling wages, fewer jobs and higher prices for basic goods ravaged the standard of living of millions already deep in poverty. As the crisis deepened and income distribution worsened, starting in the early 1980s women and children suffered most...[5]

The crisis has been exacerbated by adjustment policies imposed on developing countries in order to correct their balance of payment difficulties, resulting in considerably worsened social and economic conditions, the burden falling particularly heavily on the poor. At the same time the inability of those countries to import what they need in order to develop has caused mounting unemployment and dislocation in industrialised countries, leading to shrinking demand as those countries slid into recession, and creating a situation in which, in the words of one major Third World Women's group (DAWN), the system must 'either undergo major changes or break down', to the detriment of both North and South.

A working document prepared for an International Labour Organisation meeting in November 1987 pointed out that large imbalances in the world economy threaten its slow recovery and may perpetuate and indeed spread unemployment and poverty.

A major effort of structural adjustment needs to be undertaken by virtually all countries if these imbalances are to be overcome, and if there is to be a world-wide resumption of growth in production, incomes and employment and a decrease in poverty. Structural adjustment has, however, to be considered as a global problem since the manner in which individual countries resolve their domestic economic problems affects growth, incomes and employment in all other countries.[7]

Adjustment can be a painful process and its burden is best shared equitably both among countries and within them, says the working paper.

In particular, the poorest and most vulnerable groups should be protected against sharp falls in their levels of income and social services. Adjustment policies thus need to be designed in such a way that they lead to a growth of employment and incomes... Developing a more equitable and socially oriented pattern of adjustment requires dialogue and negotiation both at the international level and within countries, between the government and representative organisations, including those of employers and workers.

The paper emphasises that serious mistakes by many developing countries in the management of their economies were also responsible for the extremely difficult situation in which they now find themselves, but that slow growth and protectionism in industrialised countries have increased the burden of adjustment in developing countries, whose difficulties then have a negative impact on employment and incomes in countries where industries and jobs are dependent on exports to the developing world.

DROWNING **IN DEBT** ☐ The total debt of the developing world is estimated by the World Bank to have risen from $562 billion in 1982 to approximately $1,020 billion in 1988.[8] According to UNICEF, in many countries annual repayments of interest and capital amount to more than the total of all new aid and loans being received each year.

On average, repayments now claim almost 25% of the developing world's export revenues. Meanwhile ... income has declined. The developing world still depends on raw materials for the majority of its export earnings. But in the last ten years, real prices for its principal commodities – including fuels, minerals, jute, rubber, coffee, cocoa, tea, oils, fats, tobacco and timber – have fallen by approximately 30%. The fall in new commercial lending and the inadequate and static levels of official aid complete the four walls of the financial prison in which so much of the developing world has been incarcerated during the decade.

Among the public in the industrialised world, it is still widely believed that money is flowing from rich nations to poor nations to assist in the struggle against poverty. Ten years ago, that was true. In 1979 a net $40 billion flowed from the northern hemisphere to the developing nations of the South. Today that flow has been reversed. Taking everything into account – loans, aid, repayments of interest and capital – the southern world is now transferring at least $20 billion a year to the northern hemisphere. And if we were also to take into account the effective transfer of resources implied in the reduced prices paid by the industrialised nations for the developing world's raw materials, then the annual flow from the poor to the rich might be as much as $60 billion each year. For much of the developing world, the economic climate has therefore darkened quite dramatically in the last decade. As a result, most of the affected nations have been forced to adopt economic adjustment policies in an attempt to stave off balance-of-payments crises while at the same time meeting debt obligations, maintaining essential imports, and struggling to return to economic growth.'

> Asked what was the best joke he had heard in the past year, Ben Elton, a leading British comic, replied: 'Well, it was actually told to me by OXFAM - that for every pound we gave for famine relief in Africa, two pounds came back in debt repayments. That is the best joke I have heard this year'.[10]

As *Asiaweek* commented in March 1989:

> For sheer doggedness of purpose and waste of resources, the seven-year financial siege of debt-ridden developing countries has made Napoleon's march on Moscow seem in comparison a triumph. There may be other policies that have done more to lame international growth and goodwill, but it's hard to think of one. Ever since the threat of default became a red alert in 1982, insistence by creditors on payment in full has stunted some of the world's most promising economies. The Philippines today, even after three years of steady recovery, remains poorer than it was in 1981.[11]

In April 1989, 28 of Africa's poorest nations appealed to foreign creditors to write off all of their foreign debt, since most were on the verge of economic collapse. A report to a meeting of African economic planning and development ministers noted that the foreign debt of the 28 countries – among the 42 least-developed countries (LDCs) worldwide – had tripled this decade, to $40.2 billion. African countries are estimated to have $218 billion in foreign debt, mostly owed to governments. The appeal expressed concern about falling prices for commodity exports, inadequate foreign aid, hardening terms on such aid and growing debt, all aggravated by severe weather and refugee problems. 'The combination of all these factors has led to the increase in the number of LDCs in Africa from 21 in 1981 to 28 in 1988 ... debt represents 90.5% of the combined gross domestic product of the African LDCs in 1987.'[12]

MEETING IMF CRITERIA ☐ In order to avoid defaulting on their debt payments, developing countries need to raise further credit, but cannot be considered 'creditworthy' unless they accept the

International Monetary Fund's Recommendations for Adjustment. These adjustment policies are based on the concept that the forces of the market or actions by government must encourage a solution. 'Adjustment programmes seek a shift from a trade deficit to a trade surplus, or at least a reduction in size of the trade deficit, at least in part to service the debt,' explains the 1989 Update of the 'World Survey on the Role of Women in Development', prepared by the UN Division for the Advancement of Women.[13]

To achieve this, import cuts in indebted developing countries were widespread in the Eighties, particularly in Africa. Adjustment programmes also typically included exchange rate and trade policies, as well as pricing policies, aimed at shifting incentives in favour of production for export... usually combined with demand-reducing policies... Adjustment policies, as a general rule, are based on the imposition of austerity, a concept of 'living within one's means' in an aggregate sense.

Pointing out that 'the economic and social effects of debt and adjustment fall on a society where inequality between women and men is a fact', the Update suggests that 'the most profound consequence of the crisis has been to perpetuate this inequality'.

The IMF's task being to ensure a stable monetary framework for world trade and to help member countries overcome temporary problems with their balance of payments, its recommendations have tended to be of a short-term nature, unsuitable for the deeply-entrenched, long-term structural problems faced by the indebted countries. Reduced public spending through reduction of subsidies, price increases or reductions in public services such as health and education, staff cuts and limita-

tion of wage increases, restriction of money supply and devaluation of the currency in order to increase exports and reduce imports, have all exacerbated the situation in indebted countries while in no way helping their creditors; the latter have been trying to solve their economic problems by raising barriers against Third World imports, which in turn has made it more difficult for indebted countries to earn the funds required to meet their debt obligations.

Africa, which has had to cope with wars, drought and environmental deterioration as well as the impact of the debt crisis and world recession, has undoubtedly been hardest hit. According to the representatives of 30 African countries meeting in Khartoum in early 1988, adjustment programmes are rending the fabric of African society.

Structural adjustment programmes (SAPs) are incomplete...too mechanistic...and in too short a time perspective...they must be made to complement the efforts of African governments to attain their long-term development objectives. Consequently they should, through their effects on the economy and the African social fabric, contribute to the preservation of basic human rights and fundamental freedoms and help to eliminate policies that discriminate against minority and vulnerable groups.[14]

Unless action is taken to reduce it, Africa's debt service obligation in 1995 is likely to reach an impossible $45 billion; the servicing of mounting debt ensures that countries cannot maintain essential social services, invest in their future (including their future human resources), return to growth, increase their imports, or contribute to a healthier world economy.

Negative or slow growth is expected for the next few years for the group of developing economies outside Asia, says UNICEF, unless radical policy changes are introduced in the areas of debt and capital flows, or a strong recovery in the industrial market economies revitalises world trade and, with it, commodity prices. Special efforts are needed in African countries to raise agricultural productivity and food production.[15]

DEBT SERVICING □ At a recent meeting in Geneva of the UN Conference on Trade and Development (UNCTAD), the representative of the World Bank dwelt at length on the deteriorating condition of the debtor countries. He said both debt service ratios and interest service ratios are higher now – 'in some cases dramatically higher' – than they were at the onset of the debt crisis. The reverse outflow of resources, while showing 'a dramatic increase' in recent years for three regions (East Asia and the Pacific, Latin America and the Caribbean, and Eastern Europe, the Middle East and North Africa) was most pronounced in the case of Latin America, where it was expected to reach $25 billion in 1988 and a cumulative $110 billion since 1983. For the heavily-indebted middle-income countries, the rate of growth in 1987 was only about 1.6%, 'still unacceptably low.'

For Sub-Saharan Africa, the situation is so bleak that only 12 of the 44 countries have been able to service their debts regularly, which is not surprising given the fact that in 1986-87 debt service obligations amounted to over 20% of their export earnings. Paying the $21 billion due in debt services for 1988-89 would 'take too high a percentage of its projected export revenues, leaving too little to finance the imports required to make adjustment work and to promote higher growth.'

Though the term debt reduction did not appear in the statement, it suggested itself in the light of the World Bank's grim judgement that:

The volume of financial flows to developing countries is inadequate to meet their needs for economic growth, poverty reduction, structural adjustment and the resolution of their debt difficulties. Commercial lending is now very small and there is no prospect that concessional flows can compensate for this shortfall.

Summing up at the meeting, the Director of UNCTAD's Money, Finance and Development Division suggested that there would be a broad consensus on the proposition that debt reduction 'could, and indeed should, play a more important role in the strategy than has so far been the case.' The UNCTAD Report considered 'some government involvement would be required if debt reduction is to take place of a magnitude and at a pace that would make a decisive difference for debtor countries.'[16]

In a paper written for the *International Labour Review*[17] Rolph van der Hoeven analyses the effect of external shocks on the economies of developing countries – especially exporters of primary commodities and more traditional manufactures – and concludes that, in general, stabilisation efforts should be spread out over a much longer period, and form part of a long-term growth and adjustment policy.

Since stabilisation policies often involve difficult choices as to how the burden of adjusting to external shocks should be distributed, any meaningful stabilisation programme must obviously be based on a fair degree of social consensus if it is to be successfully implemented. This implies designing programmes in consultation with all the social groups that are going to be affected. It could lead, for example, to the formulation of incomes and price policies that limit not only wages but also other types of income such as profits and

rents. Furthermore, a social consensus could be sought for safeguarding a minimum level of living by exempting the lower-paid from falls in their income in times of economic contraction, and by providing a floor in the form of minimum wages and guaranteed access to essential services.

MILITARY EXPENDITURES ☐ The 1986 total of world military expenditure, $900 billion, was to be outstripped in subsequent years, with an annual expenditure of some $1,000 billion – about the same as the total debt of the developing countries. Of this amount, some 15% is spent by the developing countries, which allocate approximately 30% more to the military than to health and education combined. 'During the eleven years ending in 1985, when their external debt rose to $580 billion, developing countries imported $250 billion worth of arms (both totals in current dollars) ... equivalent to over 40% of the additional debt incurred in that period', says Ruth Leger Sivard, author of *World Military and Social Expenditures*.

Meanwhile, the boom in military spending in the developed world contributed to the accumulation of debt by inflating interest rates. In the US the military spending spree was a prime factor in the sudden rise in the budget deficit, helping to push up interest rates to record highs for dollar-denominated debt ... lenders' prescriptions for improved economic health surprisingly do not appear to include specifications for a slimming military diet. Economic advisers apparently are reluctant to intrude on matters regarded as 'national security', as though it had nothing whatever to do with the public welfare. However the enormous external debt accumulated by the Third World, and owed to the industrialised countries, is another political time bomb, with potential repercussions for rich as well as poor countries.[18]

1987 recorded a new high in global expenditures at $1.8 million a minute.... The strain on the world economy has become as ominous as the oversupply of killpower in nuclear stockpiles. A military joyride on credit has left mountains of debt for future generations. Rising poverty and the lengthening lines of the unemployed contrast with the affluence with which military programs operate. Public pressures for restraint are more vocal and insistent. Increasingly, government policies have begun to respond to these pressures.[19]

Cuts in government spending due to the world economic crisis have fallen more heavily on health and education than on the military. Between 1983 and 1986, military expenditure in developing countries (as a percentage of total public expenditures) was reduced from 6.7% to 6.1% (a 9% cut), while expenditure on education was reduced from 3.8% to 3.4% (a 10.5% cut) and on health from 1.5% to 1.3% (a 13.3% cut). A few developing countries have reduced military expenditure in response to the crisis: Zimbabwe, where the share of the military in recurrent expenditure has fallen from 44% to 28%, with education and health rising from 22% to 27%; and Uruguay, which has cut such allocations by 65.4% and is using military personnel to build schools and training institutes.[20]

SOCIAL CONSEQUENCES, NORTH AND SOUTH ☐ It is generally agreed that it is not the *need* for adjustment, but the *manner* of adjustment that is in question. The impact of adjustment measures on the social well-being of the peoples of Third World countries has been dramatic. As the social effects of adjustment processes become more apparent, it is clear that the main burden is falling on those least able to bear it – the poor and most vulnerable, especially women and children. Malnutrition is increasing, diseases are re-appearing, school enrolment rates are falling and drop-out rates rising – in short, the social progress of decades is coming to a grinding halt, or even being thrown into reverse.

The world economic crisis creates misery for people in all parts of the globe. OECD reports that over 31 million people – more than 8% of the work force – are without jobs in the rich indus-trialised countries[21], where relative and absolute poverty have emerged on an unprecedented scale. Yet it is the poor of the Third World, without even rudimenta-ry welfare systems to support them, who bear the largest burden, many of them paying with their lives. There, the impact is felt principally among the most vulnerable groups: food-deficit farming households, pastoral communities, the landless, the urban unemployed, and those with jobs that do not pay enough for survival. Where women are heads of households, the impact is even more dramatic.

An aspect that appears to have been given far too little attention in recent international meetings is the question of the extent to which the world economic crisis has been caused by discrimination against women and the fact that, in all countries, their role in the economic and social sphere has not been taken into account in terms of GNP, GDP, or any of the indices which monitor progress or decline in terms of development. Women, as citizens, have had all too little say in national development plans or in adjust-ment policies accepted by their govern-ment.

> And we, the housewives, ask ourselves: What have we done to incur this foreign debt? Is it possible that our children have eaten too much? Is it possible that our children have studied in the best colleges? Or do they wear the best clothes? Have we improved our standard of living? Have our wages become so great? Together we say: No, no, we have not eaten too much. No, we have not dressed any better. We do not have better medical assistance. Then to whom have the benefits gone? Why are we the ones who have to pay for this debt?
>
> DOMINGA DE VELASQUEZ, SPEAKING ON BEHALF OF THE WOMEN OF THE
> AMAS DE CASA OF LA PAZ, BOLIVIA[22].

Indeed, says Lucille Mair, former Assistant Secretary-General of the United Nations, if women were marginal beneficiaries in the boom times of the 1960s and 1970s, they are anything but marginal sufferers from today's debt repayments.

Women and children...are typically seen as neither economically nor politically significant enough constituencies to matter. So it is a whole range of family human services such as education, health, child care and nutrition that sink lower on the agenda of national priorities ... precisely at the time when fiscal stabilisation measures most severely curtail the purchasing power of the poor, of whom a majority are women, and household incomes decline.

In the Third World we are observing the greatest burden of the world economic recession passed on to those least able to sustain it, women, who having no public say are the least responsible for creating the fiscal mess we are in today, with its accompanying social distress, and no viable solutions being proffered either nationally or internationally...The fact is that a world managed by men has a lot to answer for when they have managed to transform the traditional food producers of Africa, namely its women, into the saddest victims of famine and food shortages.[23]

9

Without 'barefoot' businessmen, women and children many Third World cities would quite literally grind to a halt. Lima, for example, relies upon the informal sector to provide 80 per cent of its public transport, while 'illegal cities' or shanty towns provide the majority of housing for the people of Lagos and Mexico City.

The garbage pickers of Cali, the donkey-bridle-out-of-bicycle-chain-makers of Ouagadogou, the kettle-out-of-tin-can-makers of Bombay are all spontaneous pioneers of intermediate technology. They are recycling and adapting whatever materials are at hand.

Kids hawking cigarettes, women selling cooked food on street corners, feature overwhelmingly in the informal sector. Without their contributions many families would not survive. But the children's formal education suffers as they learn street wisdom instead.

The sweatshops of the Third World provide illegal employment for hundreds of thousands of people – but at a cost. Often dingy, overcrowded and unsafe, these can pay way below the minimum requirement for survival. But legal jobs are so rare that many people have no choice but to work in these conditions.

Going legal is hard. In many countries the hurdles – bribery, corruption, bureaucratic red tape – are too awesome for a small business person even to consider. A study in Peru showed it took 461 days, 24 bribe demands and 120ft of paperwork laid end to end, to register legally a small clothing workshop. The same process took under four hours in a city in the US.

The formal and informal sector often overlap – with the former generally exploiting the cheaper, non-unionized labour workforce the latter contains. Mexican electronics firms 'put out' work to women, paying them half of what they pay their regular employees. Meanwhile many struggling legal companies sell their goods under the counter – evading tax – to street-vending suppliers.

Because of social and gender discrimination, the strategies adopted for structural adjustment have not taken into account an analysis of the vital economic role of women in agriculture, in industry, and in the home. Thus, instead of supporting women's productive roles, structural adjustment programmes created further obstacles to their economic participation and consequently reinforced the negative impact of such programmes on the most vulnerable.

The issue of *Women's World* in which the above quotation from Lucille Mair appeared gave a number of basic principles for alternative solutions to the debt crisis, including insistence upon priority being given to the perspectives and projects of grassroots organisations, particularly women's organisations and trade unions.

A strengthening of power in favour of the poor is essential. The major objectives must be to increase their access to land, credit and skills and to maintain essential services – primary health care, water and sanitation and education.... Political mobilisation and people's initiatives at the grassroots level, in the North and the South, are vital resources in the quest for economic justice, nationally and internationally.[24]

It is, however, probably necessary to go further – to ensure that women are integrated into the decision-making process at both local and national levels.

The effects of this economic crisis have been superimposed upon the already serious effects of underdevelopment and of social and gender inequities which exist in general. What is in crisis is not only the economic system, that operates at the macro-level, but also the structures which people – individually and in groups – use to meet their own needs at the micro-level. In a report on the problem presented to

the UN General Assembly in September 1988, the Secretary-General said that the debt problem was global in its reality and in its consequences. 'It is a major political issue with a bearing not only on relations between the creditors and the debtors but on prospects for the world community as a whole'.

Pointing out that the development process has come to a halt in the countries of Africa and Latin America, the report indicates that most troubled debtor countries are no better able to cope with their debt problems than in 1982. 'If anything, the task of aligning debt-service obligations with capacities is much more formidable today after several years of economic retrenchment and social regression.'[25]

According to a working paper prepared for the ILO High Level Meeting on Employment and Structural Adjustment in November 1987, it is important for the resumption of worldwide growth and employment creation to mobilise a much greater effort of international co-operation – including capital flows at concessional terms for the poorest countries and the dismantling of protectionist measures – in order to assist developing countries to overcome their adjustment problems, spread the adjustment process over a longer time-span, and encourage governments to resist the efforts of special interest groups attempting to prevent necessary changes in policies.

When worldwide growth resumes, countries with a flexible and diversified production structure and with a well-trained and mobile labour force should soon overcome payments imbalances. [But] unless there is a major change of policy in the industrialized countries regarding trade, capital flows and aid, backed up by appropriate policies in the developing countries, there is little likelihood of sufficient growth to bring about fuller employment or a reduction of poverty in the developing world.

While it is important for both industrialised and developing countries to pursue
vigorously domestic policies that will
simultaneously contribute to adjustment,
higher levels of employment and greater
equity, all countries need a more
favourable international economic environment if these policies are to succeed, said
the working paper. 'The present international trade and financial system is not
functioning in the interest of any country
or group of countries.'[26]

Indeed, in his report to the April 1990
United Nations Special Session, Secretary-
General Javier Pérez de Cuéllar says that
during the 1980s the average per capita
income increase was the lowest in three
decades, and that debt continues to sur-
pass all other economic difficulties of
developing countries. Many people were
worse off at the beginning of 1990 than
they were in 1980, says the report, with
economic set-backs resulting in political
instability and unrest. 'The growth rate in
the developing countries has been insufficient to keep pace with the rate of growth
of population, implying a decline in the
average level of well-being of the peoples
in those regions.' Absolute numbers living
in poverty, as well as the number of illiterates and malnourished, increased in the
1980s. Most developing countries' spending on health, housing, education and
social services declined, and there has
been an increase in unemployment and
under-employment in most countries.

A number of important intergovernmental and non-governmental meetings
have been held in the past two years in
order to discuss the relationship of
women's issues to the debt crisis. Among
them have been 'Women and the Debt
Crisis', held in The Netherlands in March
1988; the OECD's Development Assistance Committee's 'Expert Group on
Women and Development', which met 18
April 1988 in Paris; and a United Nations

Interregional Seminar on 'Women and the
World Economic Crisis', which took place
in October 1988 in Vienna. Information
emanating from these and other meetings
has been used in the compilation of this
book, and input has also been sought from
global, national and community sources
worldwide, including case studies undertaken in a variety of countries.

1 Report available from the United Nations Non-
Governmental Liaison Service, Geneva.
2 Reported in *The Economist*, 25-31 March 1989.
3 Others have estimated this outflow at $30 billion - see
chapters 2 and 11.
4 Frances Stewart, *The Evolution of the Economic Crisis
and its Impact on the Poor*, UN/NGO Workshop,
Oxford, September 1987. See chapters on Zambia,
Mexico, The Philippines, Ghana and Jamaica.
5 S. Joekes, *Women in the World Economy*, INSTRAW,
Oxford University Press, 1987.
6 DAWN: Development Alternatives with Women for a
New Era.
7 Working document WEP 2-46-04-03 (Doc.1), High-
Level Meeting on Employment and Structural
Adjustment, Geneva, 23-25 November 1987.
8 *World Debt Tables*, Vol.1, World Bank, December
1988.
9 UNICEF, *The State of the World's Children, 1989*,
OUP, Walton Street, Oxford, OX2 6DP.
10 Quoted by John Clark, OXFAM/UK, at UN/NGO
Workshop, Oxford, September 1987.
11 *Asiaweek*, Hong Kong, as quoted in the *International
Herald Tribune*, 24 March 1989.
12 As reported in the *International Herald Tribune*, 21
April 1989.
13 Update, Chapter 11: Women, Debt and Adjustment.
14 See *The Khartoum Declaration*, Report of the
International Conference on the Human Dimension of
Africa's Economic Recovery and Development, United
Nations, Khartoum, Sudan, 5-8 March 1988.
15 Cornia, Jolly, Stewart, *Summary and Conclusions*,
Adjustment with a Human Face, UNICEF 1987.
16 UN Conference on Trade and Development, Geneva,
Doc. TAD/INF/1962.
17 R. van der Hoeven, 'External Shocks and Stabilisation
Policies: Spreading the Load', *International Labour
Review*, Vol.26, No.2 March-April 1987.
18 Ruth Leger Sivard, *World Military and Social
Expenditures 1986*, World Priorities, Box 25140,
Washington DC 20007.
19 Ibid.
20 *State of the World's Children 1989* and Annual Report
1987, Uruguay, UNICEF, New York.
21 Reported by Ruth Leger Sivard in *World Military and
Social Expenditures, 1987-1988*.
22 As cited by A. Cottringer and A. Pearson, 'Women and
the Debt in Bolivia', a project proposal.
23 Lucille Mair, 'Women in the World - the Challenge of
the Nineties'. Paper presented at the University of
South Dakota, April 1986.
24 *Women's World* No.17, March 1988, published by

ISIS/WICCE, Women's International Resource Centre, P O Box 2471, 1211 Geneva 2, Switzerland.

25 Report of the Secretary-General, *External Debt Crisis and Development: Towards a durable solution of the debt problem*. United Nations 43rd session, September 1988.

26 International Labour Organisation, Secretariat Working Paper, November 1987.

2 IMPACT OF STRUCTURAL ADJUSTMENT ON WOMEN

When we speak of the 'poorest of the poor', we are almost always speaking about women. Poor men in the developing world have even poorer wives and children. And there is no doubt that recession, the debt crisis and structural adjustment policies have placed the heaviest burden on poor women, who earn less, own less and control less.

REDUCTIONS IN HEALTH AND CHILD-CARE services mean that women must assume even greater responsibilities in these areas. Cuts in educational services usually fall on adult literacy classes for women or on the extension of schooling for girls. Where schools are closed and the distance between home and school is increased, girls, who must help with household tasks, have less opportunity for education. Elimination of food subsidies, falling wages and rising prices reduce women's spending power as food providers, and they must daily cope with the sheer survival needs of their families.

In societies the world over, women are both producers and carers; they care for children, for old people, the sick, the handicapped, and others who cannot look after themselves. They service the household with food, cleanliness, clothing, and in many cases water and fuel. As long as these jobs are done by women, they are not assigned any economic value, and their expansion is therefore taken for granted in times of economic adjustment. When food prices rise and wages fall, a woman must spend more time finding ways to satisfy her family's hunger, travelling further to cheaper shops or markets, preparing cheaper food, and often eating less herself in order to feed her husband and children.

The United Nations Interregional Seminar on 'Women and the Economic Crisis', held at the United Nations Office at Vienna in October 1988 in order to evaluate the effects of the crisis, also had as an objective the beginnings of a new approach, more scientific in nature, to the issue of the status of women, providing means for a less emotional and subjective approach to the issue. Based upon technically substantiated demonstration and on the identification of priorities, such an approach is needed if policy-makers are to be convinced that there has been a specific effect of the economic crisis on women.

Of course, such a demonstration is always confronted with the lack of reliable statistics on women's activities or, for example, on women's nutritional status. Discussions and country studies at the Seminar revealed that many aspects of the impact of the crisis cannot be measured and quantified, which appears to be due to a misunderstanding of the actual performance of women and the statistical concept of 'economic activity'. Empirical evidence provides some additional signals, however: in Asia, particularly East Asia, women have shared some prosperity, indirectly as members of households and directly by the increase in availability of paid employment. In Latin America, women and men alike have suffered declines in their living standards; women's employment prospects in Latin American manufacturing and African agriculture have deteriorated during the recessions,

FLORENCE

In a slum area of the capital [of Zambia], Lusaka, I met a young woman called Florence. Prior to the debt crisis, she would have been regarded as one of the better-off. Now she is one of the new strata, the nouveaux pauvres, and she was close to breaking point. For four years, prices of basic foods had been rising rapidly and it had become more and more difficult to survive on her husband's salary as a junior clerk in a government office. Often they had to survive on just one meal a day and they could only afford the luxury of meat on pay day.

Her two children became prone to diseases and in November the smallest developed an acute respiratory infection. The doctor prescribed a course of medicine but the clinic had run out of the drug because the government could only afford enough foreign exchange to import one-seventh of the country's requirements of essential drugs. She managed to find a chemist's shop which could sell her the medicines she needed, but at an exorbitant black market price. The family's food allowances for the week went in a stroke; she had to borrow.

At about this time she discovered that she was pregnant. This should normally, of course, have been a happy time; they wanted a third baby. But she couldn't stop worrying about how the family was going to survive. A week later her husband came home with the news that, due to the IMF austerity programme introduced to rescue the economy, the price of maize meal, the staple food, was going to double. 'When my husband told me I just couldn't believe it,' she said. 'Then I looked into his eyes and saw that it was true. Suddenly it occurred to me that we just wouldn't survive. We would all go hungry. And then I just burst into tears.'

Florence, with tears of desperation streaming from her eyes, is the human face of the debt crisis. In the event, the price rise only lasted a few days. Thousands of the urban poor in Zambia took to the streets and rioted. The government brought back the food subsidy, restoring maize meal to its previous price. Its decision caused tension, however, between the government of Zambia and the IMF who questioned the commitment of the government to rescuing the economy.

An organisation which OXFAM supports in Lusaka, the Human Settlements of Zambia, has been able to help Florence. It has set up a clinic for preventive health and supplementary feeding of the growing numbers of malnourished children... and started a kitchen garden scheme. Florence, and hundreds like her, have been supplied with seeds and shown how to grow vegetables... most families can find a bit of wasteground near to their homes to start a vegetable garden. Now just a few months later, she is growing enough vegetables not only to ensure a better diet for her family but also to sell some at the local market. In this way OXFAM, through the Human Settlements programme, is helping Florence to survive the debt crisis. But such projects can only make a small dent in such an enormous problem.

John Clark (OXFAM/UK)
at a UN/NGO Workshop in Oxford,
September 1987

while employment in other sectors has not compensated for the loss. This is especially serious because of the high incidence of female-headed households in these regions.

Case studies presented at the Inter-regional Seminar showed that the effects of the crisis on the different groups of women, and on the different aspects of women's situation (access to employment, education, health, etc.), had varied in the different countries; some insisted on the degradation in the nutritional status of women (Bangladesh), others on the lower access to technical education (Mexico), others still on increased migration (Philippines). UNICEF studies have come to the conclusion that there is a gender bias in the distribution of social costs of adjustment policies; for example, consumption, nutrition and health levels of women are lower than for men. (See Chapters 6 to 10). As a recent World Bank report pointed out:

Statistics fail to capture the psychological dimension of what is happening in Latin America. For several decades there has been forward movement in most countries. Even though poverty continued to be pervasive, more people were finding better jobs than ever before, and an increasing share of the population had access to clean water, education and medical care of some sort... The depression has brought much of this progress to a halt. Indeed, the physical deterioration in basic infrastructure, including schools and hospitals, and the mounting excess of unemployed or underemployed persons, will call for more than a weak pickup in economic growth if hopes are to be rekindled.[1]

The Inter-American Development Bank (IADB) President, Enrique Iglesias, commented in September 1988 that:

The *per capita* income of the average Latin American is 9% lower today than it was in 1980. This is the average. In some countries the standard of living has slipped back to what it was 20 years ago. It does not take much imagination to realise that behind this statistic are plummeting real wage levels, soaring unemployment (some open, some hidden), increased levels of marginality and acute poverty – in short, an erosion of every measure of social well-being. Today, one third of Latin America's population – 130 million people – live in dire poverty.

The average investment rate in Latin America in the 1970s was 24.5%. Today, it is barely 16.5%. In some, perhaps many, cases the real investment rate is not even enough to replace capital that is depleted. The resurgence of economic growth in our countries is impossible when investment rates are this low. Equally severe and just as important has been the erosion of investment in the region's people – its 'human capital' – as expenditures in health, education and nutrition have been severely cut in this decade. Unfortunately this means that the costs of this economic crisis will continue to be paid by new generations of Latin Americans.[2]

Adopting, in March 1988, its 'objectives and terms of reference', the South Commission,[3] whose members are Third World leaders (chairman Julius K. Nyerere, former president of Tanzania), commented on the world economic crisis as follows:

In the South itself, where social tensions and economic crises have become the main feature of the 1980s, there is a new consciousness that the severe deprivation and retrenchment forced on it in the name of adjustment has reached the limits of endurance. The need for purposeful domestic reform is appreciated. There is renewed emphasis on self-reliance and greater South-South cooperation as a means of coping with the South's continued victimisation by a global system in the design and management of which the South has very little say.

In the North also, there is a growing awareness that the destitution to which many Third World countries have been reduced in the wake of the debt crisis has severe disruptive consequences for the world economy as a whole. There is now a somewhat greater, albeit limited, willingness to recognise the contribution that growth in the Third World could make to a more healthy world economy, to a faster growth of international trade, and to easing the payments imbalances that exist among major developed countries.

The evolving situation thus contains a number of elements which, if harnessed properly, could provide the basis for a fresh start in the task of devising a new global system of collective economic security in which promotion of Third World development would be a key constituent. These positive and more hopeful tendencies are, however, still not strong enough to break the powerful hold of the status quo.

Speaking at a meeting at the NGO Special Commission on Human Rights in December 1988, Clarence J. Dias, Secretary-General of the Asian Coalition of Human Rights Organisations (ACHRO) and President of the International Centre for Law in Development, said that there was a need to examine more closely the relationship between development and human rights:

Extreme poverty (and its attendant powerlessness and dependency) breed widespread human rights' violations. Lack of resources seriously impedes the realisation of human rights of the poor. Yet present-day development programmes and projects aimed at generating economic growth and development have often tended to exacerbate rather than alleviate the problem. In most developing countries there is an urgent need for development and economic growth, but such development must be sustainable and such growth must be economic growth with a human face. This can only be realised if an effective human right to development is articulated and implemented.

Mr Dias deplored 'wanton indebtedness prompting the adoption of debt and structural adjustment policies which lead to food and job riots and virtual genocide for certain sections of society, including vulnerables such as children and women.' Redistributive policies could be adopted allocating a differentially large proportion of the benefits of development to the poor, he suggested, thus correcting historically skewed patterns of distribution of resources, wealth and power. Human rights could provide the means for ensuring that development will be sustainable, ecologically sound, and would not be at the expense of generations yet to be born.

EFFECT OF ADJUSTMENT POLICIES ON EMPLOYMENT □ During the 1980s women have been incorporated in growing numbers into wage labour employment under very poor conditions, while some of the Third World's most skilled women are leaving their countries to seek employment elsewhere.

The economic crisis has contributed to an even sharper visibility of the need to redefine the 'economic contribution', including 'economic activities', of women. When describing the latter, the first difficulty arises from the fact that they normally undertake multiple activities, usually classified as 'non-economic'. Major issues in measuring women's economic activity include gender-based stereotypes, the employment status of unpaid family workers, the reference period, the informal sector and rural activities. Since multiple activities of women add up to relatively long hours of work, the problem becomes particularly acute in cases where agricultural work and household tasks are not clearly defined or described.[4]

'One of the effects [of the world economic crisis] has been the lengthening of both the waged and unwaged working days, in a situation of generalised

EMPLOYMENT

"Women are one-third of the world's labour force but they tend to be employed in lower-paid occupations than men. Just as society undervalues the work women do in the home, so their skills are undervalued when applied to work outside in the world of employment." THE STATE OF THE WORLD'S WOMEN REPORT 1985

JOBS FOR WOMEN

Women as a percentage of the labour force in each region of the world in 1985.

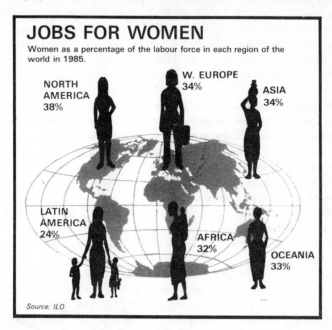

NORTH AMERICA 38%

W. EUROPE 34%

ASIA 34%

LATIN AMERICA 24%

AFRICA 32%

OCEANIA 33%

Source: ILO

UNEMPLOYMENT

When jobs are scarce women are more likely than men to be unemployed.

AUSTRALIA	6.2	8.4
FRANCE	5.6	11.7
GERMANY (FED. REP.)	6.0	7.7
ITALY	6.0	14.7
JAPAN	2.4	2.3
SWEDEN	3.0	3.4
UNITED STATES	9.6	9.4

Source: OECD

Unemployment as a % of the workforce by sex in 1982.

Unemployment figures for women underestimate the problem. In Europe only 42% of women looking for work are registered as unemployed.

Source: EEC

UNEQUAL PAY

In 1982 a woman in manufacturing industry earned only 73 cents for every dollar earned by a man doing similar work.

UNEQUAL WORK

Women tend to be employed in less well-paid occupations.

	BOSSES		SECRETARIES	
	Women	Men	Women	Men
GERMANY (Fed.Rep.)	1.3	4.2	34.0	9.6
HUNGARY	0.1	0.2	16.4	3.5
UNITED STATES	3.8	10.4	27.9	5.5
JAPAN	0.4	6.4	18.2	9.4
EGYPT	0.8	0.9	25.0	6.5
SINGAPORE	1.2	8.2	14.9	5.7
VENEZUELA	1.6	9.2	16.7	7.6

% of male and female labour force in administrative and managerial (bosses) and clerical (secretaries) jobs.

Source: ILO

uncertainty and vulnerability,' according to *The Invisible Adjustment: Poor Women and the Economic Crisis.*[5] UNICEF studies show how the crisis, and the limitations imposed by adjustment policies, have brought heavier demands on women, both within the home and outside.

They suggest that women, or the amount of labour that they do, today represent an *adjustment variable* in the context of the national efforts being made to bring the economy under control. If this essential concept were to be accepted and borne in mind, it would be possible to introduce policies based on growth and a real human dimension.

According to the proponents of a 'Women's Alternative Economic Summit',[6] the export-oriented policies required under IMF adjustment practices have increased women's participation in cash crop production and other foreign exchange activities, but at the same time have devalued the traditional areas of women's work, such as subsistence agriculture, and reinforced their marginalisation. Micro-level income-generating programmes for women have often, inadvertently, reinforced women's marginalisation from the wider economic process.

In so far as women-specific income generating and employment projects have not received the same level of resources and attention that could systematically bring them into larger macro-economic processes, they perpetuate the dominance of women in subsistence and traditional production which are more vulnerable to changing economic currents. Export-oriented policies have further alienated large segments of the population from the land, resulting in intensified land use causing heightened degradation of forests and soils. Poor agricultural workers increasingly migrate to urban centres in search of wages.[7]

But as can be seen in Chapter 6 on the effects of the crisis on the living conditions

of peasant women in Mexico, a single wage is not enough today to support a family; wives and children have to find paid agricultural employment, leading to an increase in child labour.

Declining per head food production, rising food imports, stagnant agriculture, inadequate distribution of food and resultant famines and malnutrition are clearly visible trends in several countries of the developing world. Any attempt to understand the nature of rural poverty and inequality, or to develop policies for increased food production, would have to grapple with the important role played by women in agricultural production, according to Rekha Wazir in an ILO study, *Women in a Changing World.*

Not enough work has been done on this subject to allow any generalisations, but it is clear that the relationship between land ownership and food production is not straightforward. Several questions arise on the need to study the impact of sex-egalitarian land reforms or ownership laws on:

(a) women's food production as opposed to cash crop production;
(b) allocation of time to domestic versus cultivation tasks;
(c) family nutrition levels;
(d) consumption patterns, both absolute and relative; and
(e) their participation in the sphere of decision-making and politics.

The predominance of agriculture as a major productive activity in developing countries is a well-known fact. What has been ignored in the literature on development and in census studies so far is the role women play in agricultural production.[8]

According to Mona Hammam and Nadia Youssef, in a report on a UNICEF/World Food Programme workshop, women provide the bulk of the labour required for subsistence production and an increasingly significant proportion of the labour for export and cash crops.[9]

In a study on the impact of structural adjustment on women, Elson points out

AGRICULTURE

"The evidence points to the fact that, given the same kinds of help, encouragement and incentives as men, women's agricultural productivity at least equals that of men." THE STATE OF THE WORLD'S WOMEN REPORT 1985.

DIVISION OF LABOUR

Women in Africa do up to three quarters of all agricultural work in addition to their domestic responsibilities.

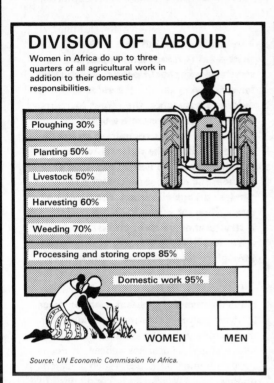

Ploughing 30%

Planting 50%

Livestock 50%

Harvesting 60%

Weeding 70%

Processing and storing crops 85%

Domestic work 95%

WOMEN   MEN

Source: UN Economic Commission for Africa.

FEMALE FARMERS

Women grow half of the world's food. But most agricultural advisors are men – who tend to give advice to men.

Women as % of agricultural advisors

Women as % of agricultural labour force

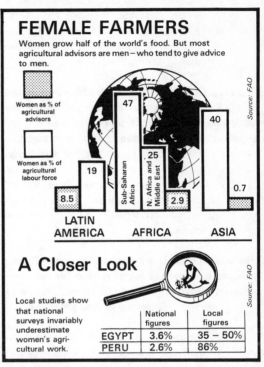

47

25 — N. Africa and Middle East

40

19

8.5

Sub-Saharan Africa

2.9

0.7

LATIN AMERICA   AFRICA   ASIA

Source: FAO

A Closer Look

Local studies show that national surveys invariably underestimate women's agricultural work.

	National figures	Local figures
EGYPT	3.6%	35 – 50%
PERU	2.6%	86%

Source: FAO

UNEQUAL SHARES

In a Rwanda village women's agricultural and domestic work take up nearly 3 times as much time as work done by men.

Source: Worldwatch Institute

LOSS OF LAND

Many women – especially in Africa – have lost their traditional rights to the land they work because colonial laws and development policies have tended to allocate land only to men.

that while there is evidence that rural producers do switch from one crop to another
in response to changing relative prices, it
is far less clear that they will be able to
increase output of a wide range of crops
in response to a general increase in crop
prices.

**There is a limit to the extent to which women can
switch from human resource production and
maintenance to crop production ... children will not
be left unattended because another crop becomes
more profitable.**

Higher yielding seeds and chemicals will
raise land productivity only if more labour
inputs, notably female labour inputs, can
be applied.

**There is an implicit assumption that more labour
time can be squeezed out of women for the more
labour-intensive practices which result from these
increases in land productivity.**[10]

The assumption is made at a time when
government expenditure on water, sewage,
health services and rural communication is
being reduced, causing women to spend
more time, or not being able to reduce
time spent, on providing goods and services of immediate use value to their families, says Ingrid Palmer in a World
Employment Programme working paper.
'Because of additional demands made on
women's time, particular support services
and investments for them are necessary if
they are to contribute to economic
growth.' Investment should be mainly targeted on women's largely uncommoditised
food production, she maintains.

**Any investments which give relief to women's work
schedule provide an external economy to other
activities ... the capitalisation of women's field
tasks has one great advantage: the necessary
investments are relatively small, and have zero
gestation period.**[11]

Ms Palmer goes on to examine the
effect of adjustment policies on population
growth.

**What can be stated at once is that all the
signs point to a pro-natal impact of
structural adjustment policies in the short
term. On every count – the value of
children's assistance, the threat to
women's personal income and the
reduction in public expenditure on health-
giving facilities – the outcome for fertility
is forbidding. More will be expected of
the household labour supply with its
gender and age allocation. There will be
competition for labour between crops...
If structural adjustment policies are to
lower fertility levels, it will have to come
through public investment in agriculture.**

ILO's *World Labour Report No. 3*, 1988,
maintains that the situation in urban areas
is deteriorating even more rapidly than
that in rural areas as a consequence of stabilisation and adjustment policies. It documents a number of issues – such as deteriorating real wages and conditions of
employment – which need more attention.
At the beginning of the 1980s, attempting
to reverse economic decline in industrialised countries, governments adopted
monetarist strategies intended to eliminate
inflation by vastly increased interest rates
and by increasing unemployment. This
has led to even less demand for Third
World products, and a steep decline in the
terms of trade for primary commodities,
which has in turn led to ever greater
unemployment in developing countries.
According to ILO research, however,
there are increased employment opportunities for women in the services sector of
many economies.

In industry, most women's jobs are con-
centrated (in both developed and developing countries) in poorly-paid, relatively
labour-intensive branches. In newly

industrialised economies such as South Korea, Taiwan, Hong Kong and Singapore, and in others such as the Philippines, Mexico and some in the Caribbean, women have been increasingly incorporated into the formal labour market because of multinational corporation participation in export processing zones. But their conditions of work and life have not improved, even where their wages are higher compared with local industries; most are young, single and semi- or unskilled, often unprotected by labour legislation or trade unions.[12]

Many Third World countries have set up Economic Production Zones (EPZs) – production sites for multi-national corporations. Attractive tax packages and a cheap, well-disciplined labour force are major inducements. There, young women are involved in labour-intensive manufacturing of electronics, textiles and footwear. The work is often detrimental to their health and there are few, if any, occupational safety standards. The *maquiladora* plants along the Mexico/US border employ over a quarter million, mostly female, workers who work 18 hours a day with few benefits and under unhealthy conditions. (See Chapter 7.)

According to a UNIDO report,[13] the employment structure of the textile and clothing industry absorbs a large number of low-skilled women workers. In almost all countries women provide the major workforce in the assembly-line jobs of both sub-sectors; in the EPZs, women often account for 90% of the total work force, employed for 'machining' garments for multinationals and the world market.[14]

UNICEF has reported that a 2-3% decline in the national income of developing countries results in at least a 10-15% decline in the income of the poorest classes. Women in the cities of Africa, Asia and Latin America are increasingly forced into the so-called 'informal' economy, as street traders, casual or seasonal labourers, domestic servants and homeworkers – unprotected by unions or employment legislation. Many, such as teachers, nurses and office workers, who have lost jobs due to austerity measures, often leave the country for domestic work in the West, or turn to prostitution – 'legal' in the sex tourism industry in South-East Asia. (See Chapter 8.) Studies suggest that there has been a deterioration in the living conditions of women from low-income sectors, often expressed in violence, the breakdown of the family, and mental health disorders. Obviously, this deterioration affects the entire family.

Analyses of structural adjustment show that the decline of formal sector employment and income has an impact on the informal sector activities of women; a decreasing family income increases the time that women spend on unpaid work, and the financial cuts in social services, education and health schemes add to their overwork. Even where women are educated and qualified, their numbers are not reflected in the labour market. Training opportunities for women in agricultural and industrial production skills are insufficient and are largely limited to traditional occupations.

A UNDP working paper on *Women and Structural Adjustment: Possible Strategies*[15] recommends adjustment policies and programmes designed for human resource development, including enhancement of women's access to education and training, self-funded sustainable local credit schemes, and public investments in water and energy supply systems as well as in transport and market infrastructure. Employment programmes, according to UNDP, should emphasise self-employment to provide income to women directly.

Inequalities between men and women in the distribution of resources, income assets and time are increasing. There is a steady impoverishment, in which women are being deprived of not only monetary resources but dignity and human rights. The economic crisis has brought multifaceted political, legal, cultural and social disadvantages to women. Unpaid work undertaken in women's multiple roles subsidises production for trade to an extent that cannot be easily quantified. Programmes of structural adjustment and the management of commodity prices take it for granted that women's time is elastic and that society can continue to benefit from their free and unpaid services.[16]

The increased time spent on production and community management activities has a distinctly negative influence on the family: child nutrition, risk of injury, child abandonment, child labour, school dropout rates (particularly among girls and children of poor single-parent families and boys who, without parental supervision, become involved in street gangs). The increase in child abandonment and deliquency is often referred to as one of the most negative consequences of the crisis in Brazil (Macedo 1987).

In the words of the UN Secretary-General (September 1988), 'development in a majority of African and Latin American countries is contingent upon the resolution of the debt crisis.' Equally dependent upon a solution to this problem is the hope of improvement in the situation of women in the developing countries, and recognition of their key role in the economic process.

EFFECT OF ADJUSTMENT POLICIES ON HEALTH, EDUCATION AND OTHER SOCIAL SERVICES □ Convergent

studies point out that, due to the world economic crisis, some human indicators are deteriorating: rising malnutrition and infant mortality rates, a rising proportion of high-risk pregnancies, and babies with very low birthweight, increased prevalence of disease, re-emergence in some countries of diseases previously thought to have been eradicated, and declining educational standards.

The 42nd World Health Assembly in May 1989, noting that worldwide economic trends had seriously hampered the efforts of many countries to reduce social inequities and, in some situations, had worsened the plight of the poor, called upon Member States to maintain the political commitment to reduce inequities among different population groups and to strengthen the infrastructure of health services. A report by the WHO Director-General in November 1988[17] pointed out that:

The level of health and the access to services that populations in the developing world can achieve are only in part within national control. The world economy, rich and poor, is so interdependent that few countries can grow, prosper, or achieve social equity with their own resources .... The income gap between the rich and poor countries is widening, and the gap between the richest of the poor and the poorest of the poor is also widening.

Finding new ways to cope with the new economic reality, says the report,

requires creativity and political skill in order to increase the participation of individuals and communities, nongovernmental organisations and the private sector in a spirit of partnership with governments.

Women are the primary health providers and the primary educators. They try to meet the health needs of their families and mould the attitudes of their children. This is so in both North and

INVISIBLE WOMEN

Women the world over are making a vast and unacknowledged contribution to the wealth and welfare of their communities – in unpaid domestic work and in small-scale business and trading activities. Often these women are household heads with sole responsibility for their families. THE STATE OF THE WORLD'S WOMEN REPORT 1985.

THE HOUSEWIFE

Domestic work is "woman's work" whether she is in paid employment or not.

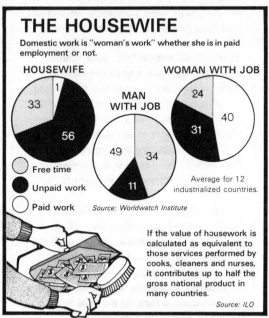

HOUSEWIFE — 1, 33, 56

MAN WITH JOB — 49, 34, 11

WOMAN WITH JOB — 24, 40, 31

Average for 12 industrialized countries.

- ◐ Free time
- ● Unpaid work
- ○ Paid work

Source: Worldwatch Institute

If the value of housework is calculated as equivalent to those services performed by cooks, cleaners and nurses, it contributes up to half the gross national product in many countries.

Source: ILO

THE ENTREPRENEUR

In many countries it is women who dominate the informal sector – the small-scale trade in goods and services not usually counted in national economic statistics.
In many Third World cities the informal sector generates up to a third of local wealth.

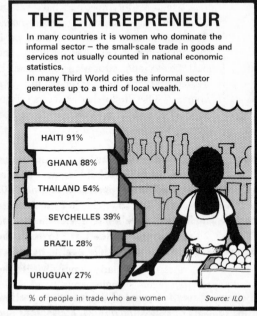

- HAITI 91%
- GHANA 88%
- THAILAND 54%
- SEYCHELLES 39%
- BRAZIL 28%
- URUGUAY 27%

% of people in trade who are women

Source: ILO

THE SINGLE WOMAN

Divorce, separation, widowhood and migration are major reasons for the worldwide increase in the number and percentage of female-headed households. Such households are among the poorest in the world.

MIGRATION

In developing countries migration is the main cause of the rise in female-headed households.

AFRICA
Sudan 22%
Kenya 30%
Ghana 27%
Malawi 29%

LATIN AMERICA AND CARIBBEAN

Jamaica 34%
Peru 23%
Honduras 22%
Venezuela 20%

% of households headed by women

Source: US Bureau of the Census.

DIVORCE

In many countries – developed and developing – divorce rates are rising and fewer couples are getting married.

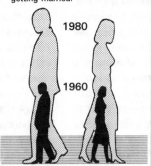

1980

1960

Since 1960 the divorce rate has more than doubled in every European country.   *Source: EEC*

WIDOWS

Because women live longer than men and tend to marry men older than themselves, more women are widowed than men,

Aged 60 – 69

Aged over 80

Figures for industrialized countries.

Source: UN World Assembly on Aging

South, but in developing countries there is less help available from social services than there is in the industrialised countries, which for the most part have national health and education programmes. When, as a result of the economic crisis and adjustment policies, government and local health and education expenditures are reduced, the first victim is the poor woman. The following excerpt from *Adjustment with a Human Face* gives an idea of the results:[18]

The growing economic imbalances and, in particular, the decline in household incomes and/or government expenditure experienced in the 1980s by 70% of the developing countries in Latin America and the Middle East, have led to a widespread and sharp reversal in the trend towards the improvement in standards of child health, nutrition, and education...

After six consecutive years of decline or stagnation, the capacity of many individuals, households and governments to resist crisis has significantly weakened, while the effect of years of poor nutrition, less accessible health care, and declining educational opportunities has accumulated to the point at which permanent damage has already been done to the physical and mental capacity of much of the future labour force. Although margins for catching up exist in many of the countries affected, it will be increasingly difficult and costly to remove the damage represented by child stunting and growing illiteracy as well as by the accumulated deterioration of the physical condition of hospitals, clinics, schools, and of the environment at large. Unless there are radical and immediate policy changes, the prediction that 'the worst is yet to come' is as valid as ever.

POVERTY, HEALTH AND NUTRITION
☐ The study lists the direct effects on poverty levels.

Besides the overall effect on poverty (tending to increase the number of people living below the poverty line) that an adjustment package tends to have, some of its specific components have a direct and unambiguous impact on particular socio-economic groups, at least in the short term. Because of the nature of the deprivations they might cause (death, brain-damaging and growth-retarding malnutrition, permanent disease-caused impairment, etc.) these effects are of a long-term nature and cannot be dismissed as part of the short-term belt tightening necessary for growth restoration. For example a growing amount of evidence indicates that:

1. Indiscriminate cuts in government health expenditure, often part of an adjustment programme, lead to declines in the health status of the population... e.g. delays in the implementation of the Expanded Programme of Immunisation in São Paulo State (Brazil) that led to an outbreak of deadly communicable diseases among children... [and] the sharp deterioration in indicators such as incidence of infectious diseases and disease-specific mortality rates in Ghana following cuts in primary health care expenditure. [See Chapter 9]

2. A radical reduction in real food subsidies in Sri Lanka, while diverting resources to investment activities as part of a new adjustment package, led to an increase in third-degree malnutrition among the children of the poorest. [And] in Chile, in 1983, the cancellation of a budget-financed child-feeding programme, part of an overall attempt to reduce the fiscal deficit, led to a statistically significant nation-wide increase in child mortality [which] resumed its downward decline as soon as the programme was reintroduced.

3. Sharp increases in food prices,

resulting from rises in producer prices or from devaluation, unless accompanied by compensatory measures, can cause malnutrition to rise among those around or below the poverty line. In The Gambia, for instance, child malnutrition increased when a Fund-Bank supported adjustment programme led to an increase in food prices without accompanying buffering measures. In general, sharp increases in relative prices of food can have devastating effects on poor households which are net food buyers. In December 1987 the Prime Minister of Zambia told the National Assembly that government, parastatal and private property worth K58.4 million was destroyed or looted during the December 1986 food riots.[19]

4. Fiscal policies typically implemented as part of orthodox adjustment are often regressive. As noted by the IMF (1986), 76% of the programmes supported by IMF between 1980 and 1983 included increases in indirect taxes and 46% in tariffs, fees and charges, as against 13% involving increases in personal, corporate and property taxes.[20]

New statistics on the well-being of the world's women, published in UNICEF's *State of the World's Children, 1989*, show the double disadvantage of being poor and female. Because in some societies female children have a lower nutritional status and higher mortality rates, they are likely to have been more affected by the general worsening of health conditions. Some half a million women die of 'maternal causes' every year. Dr Attoya Inayatullah, Pakistan's Population Minister, has put the matter succinctly:

It is intolerable that so many thousands of women are dying painful, lonely deaths in the process of giving life and we are doing so little to stop it. There is no greater indictment of development efforts than the high rates of maternal death that prevail in much of the world.[21]

Writing in the *International Herald Tribune* on International Women's Day, 1989, Dr Halfdan Mahler, former Director-General of the World Health Organisation and newly-appointed head of the International Planned Parenthood Federation, pointed out that millions of women aspire to a better life and want to participate in the development of their societies:

Yet for the great majority of women of Asia, Africa and Latin America, life consists of ceaseless physical labour and too frequent childbearing. Maternity kills half a million women each year, deaths easily avoidable if health services were adequate. A woman in Africa has a lifetime risk of dying from pregnancy-related causes 200 times higher than that of women in industrialised countries.

Evoking the case of Halima, mother of six in Niger, Dr Mahler suggested that:

We should admit how little progress we have made in eliminating discrimination against women.... The low status of women and girls is one of the most damaging, wasteful and immoral defects of society today. More than half a billion women live in abject poverty outside the development process; hundreds of millions are illiterate... Halima and her peers [must be] participants in the global effort to repair and sustain the environment in which we, the human species, must live. Without them, there is little chance we will succeed. But we have no moral right to ask for Halima's participation unless we give her hope for a better life.[22]

Adequate nutrition is also among the most obvious priorities, but as important as advances in food production is the realisation that production is only half the

DECLINE IN SOCIAL SPENDING

Adjustment to the debt crisis has forced many governments into reduced public spending. But health and education, which help to meet basic human needs now and to invest in human capacity for the future, have been cut back disproportionately.

Central government expenditure on education, health and defence, as a percentage of total government expenditure, 1972 and 1986.

	EDUCATION		HEALTH		DEFENCE	
	1972	1986	1972	1986	1972	1986
Low-income developing countries						
Bangladesh	14.8	9.9	5.0	5.3	5.1	11.2
Burkina Faso	20.6	17.7	8.2	6.2	11.5	19.2
Kenya	21.9	19.7	7.9	6.4	6.0	8.7
Malawi	15.8	11.0	5.5	6.9	3.1	6.0
Pakistan	1.2	3.2	1.1	1.0	39.9	33.9
Sri Lanka	13.0	8.4	6.4	4.0	3.1	8.0
Tanzania	17.3	7.2	7.2	4.9	11.9	13.8
Uganda	15.3	15.0	5.3	2.4	23.1	26.3
Zaire	15.2	0.8	2.3	1.8	11.1	5.2
Lower middle-income developing countries						
Bolivia	31.3	11.6	6.3	1.4	18.8	5.8
Botswana	10.1	17.7	6.1	5.0	0.0	6.4
Chile	14.3	12.5	8.2	6.0	6.1	10.7
El Salvador	21.4	17.5	10.9	7.5	6.6	28.7
Morocco	19.2	16.6	4.8	2.8	12.3	16.4
Tunisia	30.5	14.3	7.4	6.5	4.9	7.9
Turkey	18.1	11.9	3.2	2.2	15.5	13.5
Upper middle-income developing countries						
Korea Rep.	15.8	18.1	1.2	1.5	25.8	29.2
Mexico	16.4	11.5	5.1	1.4	4.2	2.5
Oman	3.7	10.1	5.9	5.0	39.3	41.2
Uruguay	9.5	7.1	1.6	4.8	5.6	10.2

Source: 'World Development Report 1988'. World Bank, Washington DC.

FALLS IN PRIMARY SCHOOL SPENDING

The chart shows that in 21 out of 33 countries for which figures are available, expenditure per primary school pupil fell, often steeply, between 1980 and 1984/85. As costs per pupil were calculated at constant prices, these falls reveal real decreases in expenditure.

Indices of recurring unit costs in the first level of education at constant prices, 1980-84/85 (1980 = 100)

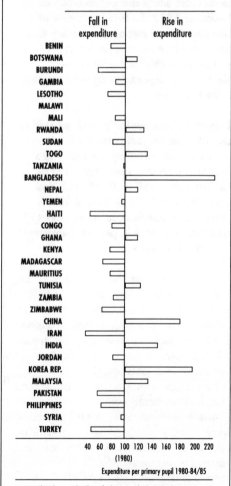

Source: 'The Educational Fallout of Adjustment' by D. Bersiecher, D & C Development Co-operation. German Foundation for International Development. Bonn. All data from UNESCO Office at Statistics.

problem. Nor is it simply a question of distribution, but of what Amartya Sen has called *entitlement* – of not having the income to buy food, or the means to grow it, or the goods to exchange for it.

Land reform, employment creation, and income levels are therefore as much a part of improving nutrition as high-yielding varieties of seed. No degree of technical advance, for example, can solve the problem that 80% of Latin America's land is owned by less than 10% of its people, or that 50% of the farm land in many parts of Asia is in the hands of less than 10% of the farmers.[23]

EDUCATION AND LITERACY □ As noted in Chapter 2 of the 1989 Update of the UN's 'World Survey on the Role of Women in Development',[24] the specific effects of adjustment policies on women's health and education are not easy to measure, since they may include reduced potential for progress which cannot easily be quantified. Where cuts in schools and educational services have been especially severe, opportunities for women in education have declined; the effects can be seen in terms of enrolment and retention rates by sex at all levels of study:

In the developing world, basic illiteracy is still a serious social problem. Over half of the adults in the Middle East, South Asia and Africa are illiterate. Despite literacy drives in many countries, the total number of illiterates continues to rise, and faster for women than for men. The lag in women's educational opportunities has wide ramifications for the development process. Not only does it mean the exclusion of a significant portion of the population from its rightful place in society's advance, but in its effect on family, health, population control and the education of children it has a retarding impact on the general pace of development... In the developed world there is growing awareness that functional illiteracy is much more widespread than progress in literacy rates suggests...[25]

Maternal education is closely related to child health, and of course to the child's intellectual development. The World Bank has characterised education as a prudent economic investment that consistently earns high rates of return, with research indicating that returns are particularly high for investment in the poorest countries. And the assurance of a minimum basic education for all has long been a major goal of development. In fact, the proportion of children in school has doubled, despite a doubling in the absolute numbers of children over the last 40 years.

But the world economic crisis, and structural adjustment measures, have had a major impact on education: the percentage of those enrolled who complete four years of schooling is now very much lower in all regions, especially for girls; drop-out rates are rising, and enrolment rates are falling, as a direct result of adjustment policies.[26] Latin American countries have reported that a high drop-out rate for women exists, due to economic factors. Scholarships are available to all, but more men take advantage of them. Included among obstacles cited that prevent women participating fully in education are lack of child-care services, shortage of crèches, distance to travel to work and education institutions, lack of social services and lack of time.[27]

A study prepared by the UN Division for the Advancement of Women found that, for a sample of 17 countries that had implemented structural adjustment policies, there was a clear tendency for a deterioration in the ratio of girls to boys in secondary education after the onset of recession, reflecting decisions by families to remove girls from schools at a faster rate than boys.[28]

In many countries there have been marked reductions in government expenditure on education, including closure of schools, with serious effects upon the educational opportunities of women and girls, especially in rural areas where transportation is inadequate and costly. Even where schools have not been closed, there has been deterioration in maintenance of facilities. In 1986 Ruth Leger Sivard estimated that one child in three aged 6–11 was still not in primary school, while for ages 5–19 the average was close to one in two. Out-of-school population is largely in rural areas or among the urban poor, with girls most affected.

Unemployment and the fall in real wages of teachers is resulting in migration from the profession. Imposition of, or increase in, school fees leads in some countries to student drop-out and a falling enrolment of women in technical and vocational education.[29] Lack of education being both a cause and an effect of women's lack of advancement, cuts in the education budget clearly retard women's progress and limit their human rights.

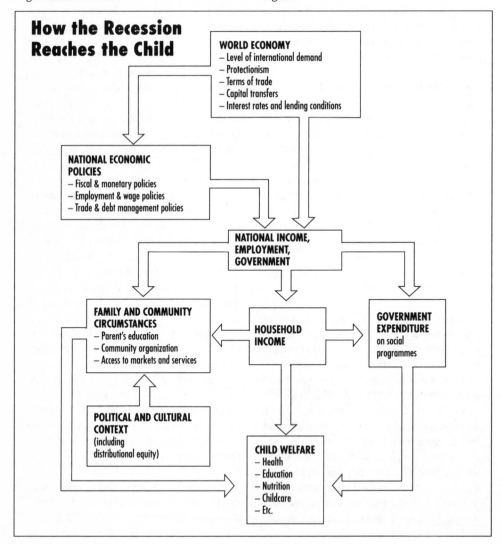

How the Recession Reaches the Child

WORLD ECONOMY
– Level of international demand
– Protectionism
– Terms of trade
– Capital transfers
– Interest rates and lending conditions

NATIONAL ECONOMIC POLICIES
– Fiscal & monetary policies
– Employment & wage policies
– Trade & debt management policies

NATIONAL INCOME, EMPLOYMENT, GOVERNMENT

FAMILY AND COMMUNITY CIRCUMSTANCES
– Parent's education
– Community organization
– Access to markets and services

HOUSEHOLD INCOME

GOVERNMENT EXPENDITURE on social programmes

POLITICAL AND CULTURAL CONTEXT (including distributional equity)

CHILD WELFARE
– Health
– Education
– Nutrition
– Childcare
– Etc.

EFFECTS ON HOUSEHOLD INCOME IN DEVELOPING COUNTRIES □ The

impact of the economic crisis has clearly resulted in falls of real household income; as food prices increase, employment opportunities drop, subsidies disappear, inflation rises, and the incomes of poor peasants and city-dwellers come under increasing, and intolerable, pressure. The situation becomes particularly acute where women are heads of families, or are left behind by husbands who look for work elsewhere. Preparing and providing food and other household needs, and generally maintaining the home with less money, fewer public services and reduced social benefits places an extra burden on women, especially when their participation in the economic field is also increasing.[30]

Efforts by households to increase their income-earning potential or change the ratio between their needs and resources include the sharing of living costs by several families in one household – economies of scale of consumption and pooling of services so that more members can become economically active – and migration, generally under conditions of severe deprivation. Out-migration of men has forcibly made the woman the major, if not the sole, supporter of rural households, and the number of women-headed households relying on insufficient and unstable remittances has grown, especially in societies where women's access to assets, credit, land, and so on is restricted. Where men migrate to rural areas they often set up other households, resulting in a declining responsibility to their families in the urban area. Urban women who have to spend more time working as well as seeking cheaper foodstuffs also find that more pressure is put on them to compensate for failure of the public system to satisfy increased demand for social services.[31]

Despite important efforts by the government of Honduras, including an Agrarian Reform Programme and the promotion of involvement of peasant women in the development process, the crisis has taken its toll in that country, and socio-economic conditions remain critical. Compounding the problem of the low land/farmer ratio are the poor quality of the land and the lack of credit and technical assistance to farmers. Some 13,865 families have deserted a resettlement area – 41% of all the families who initially settled on agrarian reform land and 85% of total desertions in the land reform programme. Peasant women are particularly hard hit: although 49.5% of the rural population, only 8% are wage-earning rural workers; 13% of all heads of families in the countryside are women with dependent children. Agencies such as UNDP, FAO and the World Food Programme have established a mechanism guaranteeing the least privileged groups of peasant women access to credit for mini-projects by means of a rotating fund.[32]

Migration of whole families normally takes place from rural to urban areas, or within the rural areas, although it can occasionally take the reverse direction; for example, the recent sharp fall in urban earnings in Accra and Dar es Salaam has provoked a return flow of migration to rural areas. But lack of employment or of possibilities in the informal sector to maintain a minimum family income, with inflation driving up the price of food and social services being cut, means that more and more people migrate to the cities or leave their countries in search of survival elsewhere.

Crisis-provoked involuntary migration is usually for both economic and political reasons. Cities throughout the world are becoming huge as people abandon their farms, while the farms are being absorbed by agri-business producing for export – which drives up the price of locally available food even more, says a report prepared for the World Council of Churches:[33]

At the same time that the debt contributes to an outpouring of people, some governments ... find themselves with far fewer resources to respond to the needs of refugees and migrants who seek security within their borders. The debt crisis means that public spending declines and resources are simply not available to provide the necessary assistance to refugee populations. Nor is the economy able to absorb large numbers of people in need of jobs.

And yet, the report continues:

Over half of the world's 16 million refugees are under the age of 16. As in the case of the human effects of the debt, children and women make up a disproportionately large number of those who are uprooted from their homes.

The authors conclude that those who work with refugees and migrants have a responsibility to address the causes which have forced so many to flee their homelands:

This work involves public education and advocacy and drawing the connections between individual situations and global politico-economic forces ... a first step in this process is to recognise that the current economic system is not neutral or value-free but is geared towards domination and dependency ... there is one 'good' thing about the debt crisis – the fact that it has brought all the mechanisms of the global economy up to the surface for all to see. This means that we can no longer say that we do not see the injustice in our world, and that therefore we can no longer avoid responsibility.[34]

Efforts to involve refugee women in economic activities have met with a number of constraints, according to a note on refugee women submitted by the UN High Commissioner for Refugees to his Executive Committee in September 1988.

Some of these constraints concern economic opportunities for refugees in general while others have particularly affected refugee women. General problems include the difficult economic situation in host countries, lack of markets, legal restrictions limiting refugees' access to work, non-availability of arable land and lack of technical expertise for project implementation.

Over and above these general problems, women particularly face problems of illiteracy and lack of education and training, cultural norms which restrict movement of refugees outside their compounds, sexual biases within refugee communities and lack of time to devote to income-generating activities. To reduce these constraints a number of steps have been taken by UNHCR and its partners. Besides providing new skills through training, traditional skills of women are exploited to produce non-traditional items for which markets can be found. In addition, women are organised to produce items at home or in all-female cooperatives.[35]

EFFECTS OF THE CRISIS IN INDUS-
TRIALISED COUNTRIES ☐ It would be wrong to assume that the world economic crisis affects only the developing countries. Quite apart from the historically high unemployment rates caused by recession in industrialised countries, domestic policies which reduce health and education budgets have caused deterioration in these services, and the number of homeless people has increased rapidly.

A study by the Urban Institute, a private agency in the United States,[36] concluded that the number of homeless people in the United States is 567,000–600,000, substantially higher than the 250,000–350,000 estimated in a 1984 report by the US Department of Housing and Urban Development but far less than the

National Coalition for the Homeless' esti-mate of three million. The Community for Creative Non-Violence in Washington has said that 'just about everyone in America who is involved' believed the figure was two to three million.

In a recent article in the *International Herald Tribune*, Spencer Rich[37] said that a special panel, funded by the non-profit William T. Grant Foundation, had report-ed that the 'forgotten half' of American youth – 20 million persons aged 16 to 24 who will never go to college – was rapidly falling into an 'economic limbo' that threatens to undermine US productivity and living standards. 'The youths are largely white, but an increasing share are black, Hispanic and Asian. A large pro-portion come from low-income areas of the south and west as well as inner-cities nationwide. At least a quarter never finish high school.'

The foundation's report, made public on 17 November 1988, sketched this por-trait of the 'forgotten half'.

Their lives as adults start in the economic limbo of unemployment, part-time jobs and poverty wages. Many of them never break free. Neglect of this segment is undermining the skills and productivity of the future labor force of this country, and therefore its future living standards. Too many people are not equipped to work. In our own selfish interests, they shouldn't be consigned to the trash heap.

In an era when jobs increasingly require more skills and are becoming more com-plex, poor income and lack of adequate education, health-care and child-care aid are major barriers to advancement, the report said. Average real annual earnings of those aged 20–24 who had not finished high school dropped 42% from 1973 to 1986. Over the same period, the propor-tion of all families headed by a person

under 25 that fell below the government's official poverty line jumped from one-sixth to one-third.

According to a 1986 US Department of Commerce report, 32.4 million people were living below the poverty line (about $8,700 a year for a family of three); 40% were under 18. Dependence on church and private sources is growing; Pittsburgh, for example, increased its emergency food centres from 50 to 250. While many of the 'supplicants' at soup kitchens are still single individuals, often homeless, two-thirds are now families, many of them designated 'the new poor'. It is clear that hunger has increased substantially in the past decade, that a growing proportion of women, children and working poor people go hungry, and that hunger is increasingly accompanied by homelessness.[38]

Among the hungry homeless, migrant farm workers are still the most wretched of workers in the United States. Often their only shelter, besides the trees, is a ragtag collection of shacks made of card-board, plastic and miscellaneous pieces of wood. Water for drinking, bathing and cooking is furnished by a hose tapped into the run-off from the nursery above. These are people from Oaxaca, Mexico; they work in the nursery and on ranches in the area, earning as little as $2 an hour.

The 1988 US immigration bill allows growers to import lower numbers of 'con-tract workers' from foreign countries, usu-ally Mexico and the Caribbean. The pro-gramme supplies employers with a perma-nently cheap supply of labour for which they pay a minimum wage, with no obli-gation to pay social security, pension or unemployment insurance. If the worker is not docile enough or does not produce enough he can, like any other bad com-modity, be returned to his home country without obligation. The losers in this pro-gramme are, of course, the farm workers, both domestic and foreign.[39]

Bleak economics and faltering farms are now creating homelessness among domestic farmers who, according to a report in the *International Herald Tribune*:

crowd into shelters in major farm-belt cities... seeking jobs and anonymity. Others head for dirt-road hamlets, where church basements and other makeshift shelters are full almost as soon as they are open.

People are living in railroad cars and tar-paper shacks... Rural people account for close to 90 percent of South Dakota's 4,000 homeless... Some of them have attempted suicide before coming into the city, because for them coming to the city means failure.[40]

A 1988 study[41] shows that in recent years the income gap between rich and poor in the United States has widened vastly more than previously understood. It points out that one-fifth of all children now live in female-headed families, twice the figure of the early 1970s, and that one-third of all such families are poor:[42]

The traditional measure shows that from 1973–1987, the last year for which data are available, the mean income of families in the poorest fifth, adjusted for inflation, rose by 11.8%. The adjusted figures show the poorest fifth losing 10.8% and the richest gaining 24.1%. For families with children (and children are now the poorest age group in society), the average income of the poorest fifth went down by 22% and the average of the richest fifth went up by 24.7%.

According to Hilkka Pietilä:[43]
Currently, 20% of children in the United States are growing up in poverty; in 1970 it was 15%. To reverse this trend a broad group of professionals armed with convincing statistics are working to maintain and expand government programmes for the poor, even during this time of economic adjustment. In the United States it has been found that:

- every dollar spent on supplemental food for pregnant women at nutritional risk saves $3 in future short-term hospital costs;
- investing one dollar in pre-natal services saves more than $3 in caring for low-birthweight infants.
- every dollar spent on immunising children saves ten dollars in later medical costs.
- enriched pre-school programmes increase performance and success of students in school later on.

An editorial in the *New York Times* said about these programmes for the poor: 'These are investments that America cannot afford not to make.'[44] Another, in the *Washington Post*, has pointed out that:

The American rate of infant mortality ranks 19th in the world, behind nearly every West European country. More than 10 of every 1,000 babies born in the United States die before their first birthday. Japan's infant death rate – lowest in the world – is half that. Some of the poorest countries do more than America to help babies survive infancy... The infant mortality rate measures more than health. It is also a measure of social attitudes and of the resolve people bring to the question of whether, in a society as wealthy as America's, children should be allowed to die for want of a relatively modest amount of regular care.'[45]

In the United Kingdom, national policy has tried to meet the effects of the world economic recession and high unemployment by privatising national assets and using North Sea oil revenues to meet benefits for the unemployed, as well as by cuts in the social services. Reductions in the education budget have led to considerable deterioration in the country's educational system and conditions for teachers, and health workers in the government's national health system went on strike for higher pay and better conditions.

"A woman's domestic role as wife and mother – which is vital to the well-being of the whole society – is unpaid and undervalued", says the State of the World's Women Report 1985.

Cartoons by Cath Jackson

Unemployment is declining, but is still high in real terms. Both men and women have been forced into the informal sector, and there is increasing poverty among the poorest.

Helen Allison has pointed out that women in Britain are

... not unfamiliar with the impact of harsh economic measures: rising unemployment, increasing poverty, drastic cut-backs in public services – health, education, social welfare, transport and housing. All reductions in public services affect women disproportionately. Although the extremes of poverty, hunger, unemployment prevalent in Latin America, the Philippines and Africa, and the sheer numbers of women, men and children affected are so far unknown to us in Britain, we can understand what is happening and raise our voices in solidarity. Action to resolve the debt crisis must start right here in Britain."

Inevitably, it is the women in Britain who have borne much of the brunt of this increasing poverty, according to Caroline Glendinning:[47]

In the first place, women have experienced attacks on their incomes and standards of living, whether derived from paid work or from state or private systems of welfare. Secondly, they have witnessed a steady erosion of their rights to work and at work, and their entitlement to an independent income when out of work. Thirdly, the quality of women's lives has been yet further reduced because economic and social policies have increased the amount of unpaid work which women are expected to perform in the home and family.

Ms Glendinning points also to the fact that, between 1979 and 1987, the two groups of women who are at greatest risk of poverty – the elderly, and lone mothers – have increased in size as a result of longer-term demographic trends:

While these increases ... are not direct consequences of government policies... the policies of the last eight years have actually increased the risk of poverty among current and future generations of elderly women and lone mothers, among others.

She underlines the fact that women's disadvantage in the labour market also affects their access to social security benefits.

These disadvantages have increased enormously; women are less likely than men, now and in the future, to be entitled to benefits at all, and are more likely to receive lower levels of benefits, than in 1979.

Child benefit – for many women the only money over which they have complete control, and essential in meeting their children's needs – was cut in value in 1980, made good in the 1983 election year, and cut again in 1985 – a cut which has not been reversed. 'Women also stand to lose considerably from the measures in the 1986 Social Security Act, both in the immediate and the longer-term future. The almost complete invisibility of women in both the Green and White Papers which preceded this legislation was remarkable,' says Ms Glendinning.

Almost half of all lone mothers currently receive SB (supplementary benefit) ... as a cash benefit payable to women, rather than as a [male] wage supplement [but] much of its increased value will be cancelled out by cuts in housing benefit and the loss of free school meals... Official figures also show that the poorest working lone parents will be worse off despite the extra resources going into family credit...

545,000 children whose parents currently claim FIS [family income support] or who are on a very low income will lose their entitlement to free school meals. The increase in family credit equivalent to 60p per school

"Domestic work is not the only work women do", says the State of the World's Women Report 1985. "There are relatively few women anywhere in the world who can claim to be 'just a housewife'."

Photo : Janine Wiedel

day will be too low to buy a secondary school meal in over half the local education authorities in the country; other families on low incomes will receive no compensation at all. Again, it is women who will be responsible for making ends meet on a reduced income; who will suffer yet more job losses and cuts in hours in the school meal service; and who will have additional unpaid work at home making packed lunches for their children.

C. GLENDINNING, 'IMPOVERISHING WOMEN'

The replacement of SB single payments by loans recoverable from future benefit would place enormous pressures on women already having difficulty in budgeting on an inadequate weekly income, while carers of elderly and displaced people, overwhelmingly women, would be the only group to lose the higher long-term rate of supplementary benefit and not receive a 'client group' premium in compensation.[48]

In a paper written for a meeting in Dublin in July 1987, Jane Millar of the University of Ulster pointed out that in recent years there had been much discussion with regard to the 'feminisation of poverty':

The phrase implies a process of change has been taking place, that the burden of poverty has shifted from men to women. Certainly women's poverty has become much more *visible* in recent years. This is partly because of demographic changes (in particular the growth in the number of lone mothers and lone women pensioners – both groups very vulnerable to poverty and both visible in poverty statistics because they often form separate households), partly because of economic changes (in particular the increase in the proportion of married women in employment – often in low-paid jobs), and partly because of feminist research which has attempted to open up the "private" world of the family.[49]

Poverty is not gender-neutral, said Ms Millar. Women are much more vulnerable

to economic insecurity and poverty than are men. Given the economic and social disadvantages experienced by most women in most societies, and the burden of unpaid work which falls mainly on women, it is hardly surprising to find that this is the case:

It is women who bear the brunt of managing poverty, often reducing their own consumption to protect their children and partners from the effects of poverty ... not only is no recognition given to the way in which the unpaid labour of women contributes to the living standards of the family as a whole, but also there is no recognition of the very low material reward that women receive in return for their work.

According to British Census figures, fewer than one in five women are married, of working age but not economically active, and thus wholly dependent on a male breadwinner. 'Most married women are in employment – either full-time or more often part-time – and contributing an important component of the family income... it has been estimated that families living in poverty would increase at least three-fold if married women were not employed', says Ms Millar. Women's needs are inadequately covered by British welfare provisions – indeed, in recent years changes in British social security provisions mean that women's access to benefits is becoming even more limited. She points out that there are currently about one million lone parents in the UK caring for one and a half million children and that nine out of ten of these are women, well over half of them living in poverty.[50]

Countries in Eastern Europe are also suffering from the impact of the world economic crisis. The too-rapid repayments of Romania's debt led to severe impoverishment of the population, exacerbated by the government's 'systematisation plan'. This involved the destruction of thousands of villages, whose inhabitants had to move into inadequate low cost housing. The immediate impact of these measures included the elimination of home-based food production, which in the course of the last few years had played a key role in avoiding starvation, and a disruption of the traditional social fabric of rural communities. As a result, village women became consumers instead of producers, and lost their socio-economic independence.

At the same time the intended 'Romanisation' of large ethnic minorities would deprive large numbers of minority children, especially girls, of adequate education or vocational training, and aggravate social problems by making it necessary for minority youth to take up employment hundreds of kilometres away from their families. At the time of writing (early 1990) the dislocations and instability following the recent revolution in Romania may, at least temporarily, add to the difficulties of the Romanian people, but the 'systematisation' and 'Romanisation' programmes will no doubt be discarded under a democratic government.

POSSIBLE CONSEQUENCES OF ADJUSTMENT FOR WOMEN AS CITIZENS ☐ The impetus given by the United Nations Decade for Women continues to have positive effects on the legislation and structures which enable women to contribute more fully in the economic and political arenas of their societies. Nevertheless, it is more than possible that the effect of the world economic crisis on women's role as citizens will be a negative one, particularly among poorer groups. Conditions which make them the first to lose their jobs in times of high unemployment, and require them to spend more

time feeding and caring for their families in the absence of adequate social services, are more than likely to reduce the role they are able to play on the national and local community scenes.

Thus, recession and adjustment may have influenced access to power, in that economic difficulties may lead women to withdraw from public activities. The process of implementing policies foreseen by the UN Decade for Women has to take into account all parties in economic and social decision-making, and all levels at which public action takes place. This means strong involvement of women in labour unions, trade associations and economic institutions. It also means that where the locus of implementation is at the local governmental level, efforts must be made to ensure women's participation, particularly where traditional practices in the past have limited it. This can be especially valuable when one is dealing with rural women in the context of the kinds of programme, investments and infrastructure necessary to improve their ability to raise food and generate income.

As at 15 June 1989 there were 98 states parties to the CEDAW (Convention on the Elimination of All Forms of Discrimination Against Women), which was adopted by the UN General Assembly in 1979 and came into force in 1985. This and other legal instruments can be used to encourage equal participation by women within existing legal structures, both as a tool for drawing the attention of decision-makers to women's rights and as a legal remedy. The point is to make women aware of their rights under these conventions and assist them to use these instruments to reach decision-makers.

The United Nations Interregional Seminar on 'Women and the Economic Crisis', held in Vienna from 3 to 7 October 1988, identified the different types of effects of the crisis as applying specifically to education, health, employment and social policies. Case studies highlighted the need to ensure that women's interests are taken into account during the design of adjustment projects, and to emphasise the role women must play in the process, since they work in sectors of key importance for adjustment.

Programmes designed for women should, according to the case studies, have three goals: to mitigate the effect of recession, whether or not fostered by adjustment; to achieve the longer-term objective of enhancing women's role in the economy; and to promote women's participation. In fact, participation was one of the key solutions proposed by the case studies, with women's organisations as the focal point for development projects dealing with women; women should be involved in the design of structural adjustment packages, since their role in the key sectors for adjustment makes them the central figures in the process.

Indeed, it would appear that the crisis has been an incentive for governments to create national institutions which promote the advancement of women, and that recent economic developments have led governments to strengthen their structural actions for women. But among the still largely unrecognised issues is that relating to the fact that improvement in productivity is often achieved at the expense of a considerable increase in women's unpaid work, which is, of course, not reflected in a country's gross domestic product or its GNP. This constitutes a hidden economic factor resulting in even more exhausting and unrecognised contributions from women. When health services are reduced, more responsibility for health care falls upon the woman in the home. When the men leave to find work elsewhere, women have to take over their work in the fields in addition to their own and this, because it is performed by women, is not recog-

nised in the national economy.

Another factor is that one effect of the crisis may be an increase in the incidence of offences and crimes perpetrated against women. The existence of increased violence, while it cannot be regarded as a direct effect of the crisis, is nevertheless the result of the combination of persistent socio-cultural factors together with conjunctural economic and psycho-social factors.

A working paper prepared by the UN Division for the Advancement of Women for its Interregional Seminar cites some of these factors:

Economic hardship, increasing pauperisation and financial instability ... contribute to the emergence or aggravation of psycho-social factors which render the level of frustration fairly high and allow for a feeling of helplessness, which can degenerate into either apathy or aggression. These are often associated with alcohol or drug abuse and hence make the financial situation of the family worse and end in a deterioration of interpersonal relations.[52]

In Caroline Moser's sub-sample among women in Ecuador, 48% said there had been an increase in domestic violence, 'identifying this as the direct consequence[53] of lack of sufficient cash, stating that it always occurs when the women had to ask for more money.' The UN/DAW working paper also speaks of another kind of violence:

If prostitution is viewed as another form of violence against women, the various economic and psycho-social factors resulting from the crisis appear to play a major role in the increase... and the flourishing, of the trade in women. Those who enter prostitution voluntarily

usually lack other sufficient economic opportunities to support themselves and their families at a reasonable level: they use it as an instrument to overcome the increasing poverty.

More research is required to define to what extent these aspects are due to the world economic crisis, as well as into the proposition that discrimination against women is not only a result of under-development, exacerbated by the world economic crisis, but one of its major causes. At the UN Interregional Seminar it was pointed out that pre-existing inequalities have caused the crisis to have a stronger impact on certain groups of women; for example women work in sectors which are especially vulnerable to the crisis, and have reduced access to education because in certain societies parents think it is more useful and more economically justified to educate boys. Some women eat less than men because they feed husbands and sons first, and are disproportionately represented among the poor. However, the general lack of statistics makes it difficult to assess the exact impact of the crisis upon them.

In spite of all their disadvantages, women are doing an extraordinary amount to overcome the problems caused by recession and structural adjustment policies. Chapter 5 outlines some of the ways in which women are surmounting their difficulties, while Chapters 6 to 10 show what is happening with regard to women in Zambia, Mexico, The Philippines, Ghana and Jamaica.

1 As reported in *The State of the World's Children, 1989*, UNICEF, New York.
2 The 1989 riots in Venezuela, in which 375 people died, were considered by the government to be a direct result of adjustment policies.
3 The South Commission Secretary-General is Manmohan Singh, South Commission Secretariat, Geneva.
4 ILO/INSTRAW, *Women in Economic Activity: A Global Statistical Survey (1950-2000)*, June 1985.
5 *The Invisible Adjustment: Poor Women and the Economic Crisis*, UNICEF, The Americas and the Caribbean Regional Office, April 1987.
6 *The Global Economic Crisis, Structural Adjustment and the Fate of Women*. Women's Alternative Economic Summit (Task Force draft concept paper), July 1988.
7 Ibid.
8 Rekha Wazir, ILO Consultant, in *Women in a Changing World: A Decade of Action.Women at Work* special issue, ILO Geneva, 1985.
9 M. Hammam, and N. Youssef. 'The Continuum in Women's Reproductive Roles: Implications for Food Aid and Children's Well-being', *Food Aid and the Well-being of Children in the Developing World*, Report of a UNICEF/World Food Programme Workshop, New York, 25–26 November 1985.
10 D. Elson, *The Impact of Structural Adjustment on Women: Concepts and Issues*, Paper presented to the Development Studies Associated Annual Conference, Manchester, 1987. As quoted in Ingrid Palmer (see Note 11).
11 I. Palmer. *Gender Issues in Structural Adjustment of Sub-Saharan African Agriculture and Some Deomographic Implications*. Working Paper No. 166, World Employment Programme Research, ILO, November 1988.
12 World Labour Report No. 3, 1988. International Labour Organisation, Geneva.
13 UN Industrial Development Organisation, *The Role of Women in Industrial Development*, Vienna International Centre.
14 Ibid.
15 Prepared by the Division for Women in Development of the UN Development Programme, United Nations, New York. SWEC/1988/wp. 11, 3 October 1988.
16 Ibid.
17 Report by the Director-General:*Global Review of the Economic Situation and its Repercussions on Health Status, Health Care Services and Policies*. World Health Organisation, EB83.INF. DOC./1, 14 November 1988.
18 Giovanni Andrea Cornia, 'Economic Decline and Human Welfare in the First Half of the Eighties', *Adjustment with a Human Face*, UNICEF, 1987.
19 *Zambian Mail*, 11 December 1987.
20 UNICEF, *Adjustment with a Human Face*.
21 Statement at the International Safe Motherhood Conference held in Nairobi, Kenya, in 1987.
22 Halfdan T. Mahler, 'International Women's Day: A Case in Point', *International Herald Tribune*, 8 March 1989.
23 UNICEF, *State of the World's Children, 1989*.
24 UN Office at Vienna, CSDHA, Division for the Advancement of Women.
25 Ruth Leger Sivard, *World Military and Social Expenditures, 1986*.
26 Report of the Secretary-General: *Equality in Economic and Social Participation*, Commission on the Status of Women, 33rd Session, 29 March–7 April 1989.
27 *Effects of Economic Recession on Women's Access to Education*, Working Paper No. 7 prepared for the UN Interregional Seminar, 3–7 October 1988.
28 Ibid.
29 Report on the UN Interregional Seminar, UN Division for the Advancement of Women, UNOV/CSDHA, Vienna.
30 Ibid.
31 See C. Moser, *The Impact of Recession and Structural Adjustment Policies at the Micro-level: Low Income Women and their Households in Guayaquil, Ecuador*, UNICEF, New York.
32 *Women in Development*. Project achievement reports from the UN Development Programme, June 1988.

33 E.G. Ferris and L. Jones, *International Debt and Refugees*. World Council of Churches, 150 Route de Ferney, 1211 Geneva 20.

34 Ibid.

35 'Note on Refugee Women', UNHCR Exec.Com. Doc.A/AC.96/XXXIX/CRP.1, 30 September 1988.

36 *International Herald Tribune*, 5–6 November 1988.

37 Washington Post Service, *International Herald Tribune*, 19–20 November 1988.

38 *New World Outlook*, June 1988. United Methodist Church, Cincinnati, USA.

39 Ibid.

40 Isabel Wilkerson, New York Times Service, *International Herald Tribune*, 3 May 1989.

41 The Green Book, published annually by the US House Ways and Means Committee on spending programmes under its jurisdiction which include most of the main federal programmes for the elderly and poor.

42 As reported in an editorial in the *International Herald Tribune*, 25 March 1989.

43 Secretary-General of the United Nations Association in Finland.

44 Hikka Pietilä, *The North is the South's Problem: Are Western Economic Thinking, Patterns and Policies a Trap for the Developing Countries?* Finnish United Nations Association, Helsinki.

45 Reprinted in the *International Herald Tribune*, 21 April 1989.

46 H. Allison, *Challenging the Debt Crisis*. SPARERIB, March 1987.

47 C. Glendinning. 'Impoverishing Women'. From A. Walker and C. Walker (eds), *The Growing Divide: A Social Audit, 1979–1987*. Child Poverty Action Group, London, 1987.

48 Ibid.

49 Jane Millar. *Uncovering Women's Poverty: A Critique of Poverty Research in Britain*. Paper for the Third International Interdisciplinary Congress on Women, Trinity College, Dublin, 6–10 July 1987.

50 Ibid.

51 United Nations Interregional Seminar on Women and the Economic Crisis. *Impact, Policies and Prospects*, October 1988. Final Report, UNOV/CSDHA Division for the Advancement of Women, Vienna.

52 *Possible social consequences of the economic crisis: increased violence in the family and in society*. Working paper prepared by the UN Division for the Advancement of Women for the UN Interregional Seminar.

53 C. Moser, *Impact of Recession and Structural Adjustment at the Micro-level: Low Income Women and their Households In Guayaquil, Ecuador*. Part 1, 1987. UNICEF Regional Programme for Women in Development of the Americas and Caribbean Regional Office, Bogota.

3 INTERNATIONAL & GOVERNMENT POLICY RESPONSES

The efforts of many countries to implement the objectives of the United Nations Decade for Women were undermined by a series of grave economic crises that have had severe repercussions, especially for many developing countries because of their generally greater vulnerability to external economic factors as well as because the main burden of adjustment to the economic crises has been borne by the developing countries, pushing the majority of them towards economic collapse.¹ The worsening of the social situation in many parts of the world, and particularly in Africa ... had a great negative impact on the process of effective and equal integration of women in development. This... reflects the lack of implementation of relevant United Nations conventions, declarations and resolutions in the social and economic fields, and of the objectives and overall development goals adopted and reaffirmed in the International Development Strategy for the Third United Nations Development Decade.²

CHAPTER 2 HAS SHOWN the inadequacy of conventional approaches to adjustment from the perspective of protecting the vulnerable and promoting growth. In many countries the position of the poor has worsened during adjustment, with deterioration in nutrition levels and educational achievement. Investment rates have frequently slowed or fallen. With reduced expenditure on both human and physical resources, the prospects for economic growth in the medium term have worsened.

THE 'HUMAN FACE' STRATEGIES ☐
It is clear that alternative adjustment packages are needed. Some countries have managed to avoid many of the negative effects typically associated with adjustment and succeeded in maintaining and even improving standards of health and nutrition, resuming growth after only a short time. Botswana, South Korea and Zimbabwe have all followed conventional but relatively expansionary *macro* policies, protecting the needs of the poor by measures to sustain their incomes and to reallocate resources to basic health and education. Botswana has placed great emphasis on employment creation through public works, and South Korea has also made use of public works to maintain incomes during economic recession.

In Zimbabwe, credit, marketing and supplies have favoured small-scale farmers, whose marketed production in consequence surged from 10% of the total in 1980 to 38% in 1985. Total government expenditure increased by over 60% in real terms from 1980 to 1984; the share of education and health in the total rose from 22% to 27% while the share of defence in recurrent expenditure fell from 44% to 28%. Preventive medicine rose from 7.6% to 14% in total health expenditure, and the share of primary education in total educational expenditure nearly doubled from 32% to 58%.

The experience of these three countries provides some important insights into how to achieve a satisfactory alternative, and demonstrates that it is possible to adopt adjustment policies which succeed in protecting the vulnerable while restoring growth. In the short run it is possible to protect the vulnerable without economic growth by careful policy interventions targeted towards the poor and needy. But prolonged economic stagnation undermines the possibility of sustaining the position of the poor, as the experiences of Ghana and Jamaica indicate (see Chapters 9 and 10). Consequently, the restoration of economic growth in the medium term must be a critically important part of achieving adjustment with a human face. Moreover, the health, nutrition, and education of a nation is one of the most important determinants of its economic potential.

It must, however, be stressed that adjustment must take place in the industrialised countries, and in the international system, as well as in the developing economies. External imbalances arise from the interaction between a national economy and the world economy. Major national imbalances may emerge from changes in the world economy without any deterioration in domestic economic management. Large changes of this sort occurred in the 1980s, for example, a fall in commodity prices, a rise in interest rates, a fall in the market for manufactures, or a decline in capital inflows.

However, viewed from the perspective of international economic management, the appropriate adjustment may be not so much in the national economies, where the major and unsustainable imbalances emerge, but in the international conditions which gave rise to them – i.e. in the factors determining the world level of demand, commodity prices, interest rates, capital flows, etc. The extent of adjustment needed at the national level then depends on how far international conditions change. UNICEF considers that the need for adjustment in international conditions is of paramount importance because, for many countries, the extent of adjustment required under present conditions is clearly excessive, and for some may not be possible without intolerable sacrifice, not only of human and social conditions but also of democracy.

UNICEF has suggested the following major elements in adjustment with a human face:

1. More expansionary *macro policies* to sustain levels of output, investment, and satisfaction of human needs over the adjustment period, gradually moving to acceleration of development. This typically implies a different *timing* of adjustment, with more gradual correction of imbalances, requiring more medium-term external finance.

2. *Meso policies*‡ designed to help fulfill priorities in meeting the needs of vulnerable groups and promoting economic growth, in the context of limited resources. These would include policies towards taxation, government expenditure, aid, credit, foreign exchange, and asset distribution, which together help determine the distribution of incomes and resources. Since the resource constraint which has always faced developing countries is greatly tightened by the requirements of adjustment, there is a correspondingly greater need to improve the allocation of resources. Priorities include those expenditures and activities that help maintain the incomes of the poor and contribute to the production and delivery of the basic goods and services they need, as well as investments and other imports essential for growth.

3. Sectoral policies to achieve restructuring in the *productive* sector within any aggregate level of resource availability; promoting opportunities, resources and productivity in the small-scale sector, both in agriculture and in industry and services.

4. Policies designed to increase the equity and efficiency of the *social sector* by redirecting effort and resources from high-cost areas, which do not contribute to basic needs, towards low-cost basic services, and by improving the targeting of interventions. Active support for a new range of initiatives which mobilise people for health and education, and for greater community action in such areas as housing, water and sanitation.

5. *Compensatory programmes* to protect the basic living standards, health and nutrition of the low-income group during adjustment, before restructuring of production and economic growth have raised output and incomes sufficiently to enable the most vulnerable to meet minimum acceptable standards.

6. *Monitoring* of the living standards, health and nutrition of the vulnerable during adjustment on a regular basis (quarterly for some items, as with much economic data), processed speedily so that progress can be assessed and the design of programmes modified accordingly. Monitoring of human dimensions should be given at least as much weight as monitoring monetary variables.

Giving clear priority to protection of vulnerable groups both in the short and medium run has important implications for the design of adjustment policies, says UNICEF. In general, it requires a less deflationary approach and more access to finance, secured either by borrowing more or deferring payments on existing debt. Macro-policies should explicitly consider the effects on vulnerable groups; expenditures and incomes should be grouped into priorities and all policy instruments aimed to achieve the chosen priorities within a given resource constraint. This requires national mechanisms to incorporate concern for vulnerable groups into policy formation, and measures to increase their empowerment and participation while restoring growth.

SMALL FARMERS: INCREASING PRODUCTIVE CAPACITY Among the structural adjustment strategies recommended by United Nations agencies is the need to give greater support to rural women. Despite the acknowledged predominance of women in agriculture in many parts of the world, women continue to be left out of agricultural strategies. In Africa, *85% of rural women are involved in agriculture,* *where they produce and process as much as 80% of family food consumption.* Reduction in male wage employment and increasing landlessness have led to increased dependence on women's earnings in poor rural households. Where successful structural adjustment requires improving the balance of payments with regard to agricultural exports and food imports, then women must be part of that strategy. There are clear linkages between structural adjustment objectives to increase food supply, the economic and technical roles of women, and the welfare of children.

Many households in both Asia and Africa are headed by women, representing some of the poorest units. In Africa there are a growing number of households where the male is absent through out-migration. In Lesotho and Botswana men seek employment in South Africa. Less-favoured peripheral areas of Zambia also have high rates of male out-migration. Most project and settlement schemes have denied women title to land, and women generally lack power, assets and participation in formal institutions to make their views known and take their share of available resources. When given the opportunity they are vigorous entrepreneurial agents but often require a strengthening of their own organisations, such as savings groups, trade associations and credit networks.

Resources have been directed towards men even in situations where women are the technical experts in crop production, as shown by research on irrigated and swamp rice in The Gambia, and subsequent investigations have confirmed this in other rice-growing African countries. Swamp rice cultivation in The Gambia is traditionally carried out by women, but when new projects were designed, the project management discussed proposals with men, not women.

Men were invited to take part in the construction work under food-for-work programmes so that the immediate benefits accrued to them. Because of the nature of 'separate purses', no benefits were received by the women. As a result they had no interest in cultivating the new swamps because they had lost their traditional control over the crop, and because the siting and construction of the swamps, lacking their expertise, made their labour input especially high. When the project management involved women by asking their advice, they were impressed by women's all-round technical knowledge of rice cultivation and water control. As a result, some modifications have been possible in swamp construction and the provision of credit to women to enable them to purchase inputs.

SUPPORTING PRODUCTIVE EMPLOY-MENT Public works schemes have provided a very large amount of employment, secured in general by low-income workers (the target group), but have been criticised for enhancing long-term inequalities and doing little to improve the position of vulnerable groups in the medium to long term, according to Frances Stewart in the UNICEF study. But there are enough examples of schemes which have significantly improved the long-term prospects of low-income groups to show that this is possible if the schemes are properly designed and controlled (see Chapter 5). Labour-intensive public works schemes can play an important role in maintaining incomes and improving economic and social capital during the adjustment process. Participation of target groups in design and control of projects is an important element in securing worker commitment, and responsiveness of the project to their long-run needs.

COMPENSATORY PROGRAMMES Governments faced with proposed adjustment programmes that are likely to have negative effects on the poor in general and their nutritional status in particular may either modify them or introduce compensatory programmes alongside the adjustment measures. Such interventions are necessary because, according to a 1986 World Bank report, 'economies cannot be expected to grow quickly enough to eliminate the chronic food insecurity of some groups in the near future, even under the best of circumstances.'

Governments may choose from an array of compensatory programmes and policies. If the aim is to compensate for losses in household incomes, then income generation, income transfer and price subsidy programmes are the most obvious choice. Food price subsidies may be used to make food or certain food commodities cheaper relative to other goods, and nutrition education and primary health care programmes may play a major role.

Income-generating programmes can include public works, food-for-work, employment generation, informal sector support, expansion of subsistence food production including home gardens, and programmes to increase agricultural production and small-farm incomes. Income-transfer measures can include food stamp programmes, poverty relief and unemployment compensation. Food supplement schemes can include on-site feeding schemes, take-home schemes, and nutrition rehabilitation centres.

In Uruguay, faced with a report that 30% of children under one year of age receiving treatment from the Ministry of Public Health were suffering from malnutrition, the government put into action a National Complementary Food programme aimed at the groups that are most vulnerable in nutritional terms: pregnant women, nursing mothers, infants and pre-school children. It has reduced military spending by 65.4%, and is using military personnel to build schools, kindergartens and training institutes.

PROGRAMMES FOR WOMEN AND GIRLS UNICEF sees women as active agents in programme delivery: as organised groups playing significant roles in managing community resources and making decisions governing resource allocation; and as individuals serving the community as health and nutrition agents, water and sanitation monitors, adult literacy trainers and family motivators.

UNICEF should help to support and/or expand their active role as producers, managers, educators, health agents, income earners, etc. (and) maximise the benefits derived by ensuring that services reach them and by supporting their participation in the planning and management of service delivery.

Education is seen as a prerequisite and key factor in raising women's awareness and empowering them to become active participants in the national development process.

A priority concern of the UN Development Programme (UNDP) is to ensure the integration of women as participants and beneficiaries in all its development programmes and projects, not only because women are significant contributors to economic and social development, but also from the conviction that sustainable development is possible only if women are more effectively involved. In this it encourages concrete action related to commitments accepted by governments when they unanimously adopted the 'Forward-Looking Strategies for the Advancement of Women' at the culminating conference of the UN Decade for Women in Nairobi in 1985.

UNDP staff are being trained in 'Women in Development' (WID) workshops and seminars and through WID sessions in regular staff training, directed at all levels of management and including,

where possible, staff from other members of the UN family. One-page country profiles are being developed by the Division for Women in Development, with a newsletter produced in English, French and Spanish – WIDLINK – to encourage information exchange and networking among UN and non-governmental organisations.

MONITORING AND STATISTICS Action is needed to establish an institutional network at the national level which will ensure that relevant data are collected, coordinated and disseminated as an intrinsic part of day-to-day operations. At the international level, national governments should be encouraged to collect, disseminate and use appropriate statistics; to publish comparable statistics on the human dimension across countries so as to permit comparisons and analysis; to use indicators in country assessments, resource allocation and national policy dialogues; and to provide early warning internationally.

A number of international institutions have taken action to monitor situations of concern to them, including WHO, ILO and the World Bank. FAO has a Global Information and Early Warning System related to problems of food supplies and famine, and actively assists a number of countries in developing national early warning systems. Extension of the FAO system to economic crises, with greater use of data on the human dimension, could provide the basis for both national and international early warnings of social stress.

Those institutions concerned with adjustment policies should have the greatest concern with the human consequences of those policies, as well as having the greatest short-term leverage, in UNICEF's view. The most effective international action would therefore be that the human dimension of adjustment be incorporated

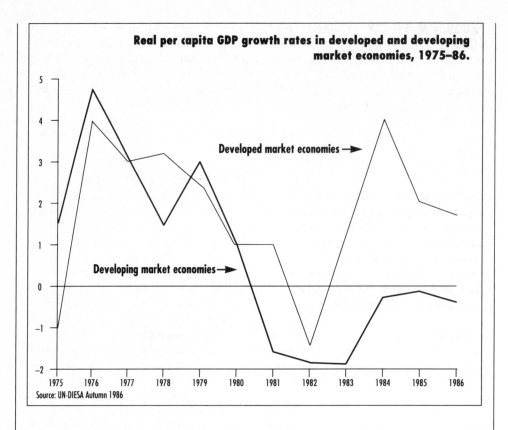

Real per capita GDP growth rates in developed and developing market economies, 1975–86.

Developed market economies ➔

Developing market economies➔

Source: UN-DIESA Autumn 1986

as an intrinsic aspect into policy dialogue and policy requirements of the IMF and of the World Bank, with appropriate statistics being a requirement for the identification of appropriate policies and for programme monitoring. As a short-term financing institution the Fund could appropriately include indicators of short-term change in the human dimension and in social stress as part of its monitoring of adjustment, while data on the condition of vulnerable groups could be an integral element of World Bank activity, more concerned with establishing statistical systems in the longer term. From an international perspective, says UNICEF, the statistical requirements of adjustment with a human face will be effectively promoted only when the need for this type of adjustment strategy is fully incorporated into the

activities of the major international financial institutions.

THE ROLE OF FINANCIAL INSTITU-
TIONS ☐ Structural adjustment programmes insist upon strong export and market orientation, and yet everyone – including the World Bank and the IMF – agrees that prospects for commodity prices are extremely bleak for the next few, possibly 10, years. Thus, a strong insistence on commodity-based export drives to stimulate economic growth would seem to be totally misplaced. It has become vital to explore different approaches to structural adjustment, both for the policy design and for the process itself.

The World Bank plans to double its lending for population, health and

nutrition as part of a six-pronged programme to improve the lot of women in
the developing world, said President
Barber Conable at the Safe Motherhood
Conference, co-sponsored by the Bank,
WHO and UNFPA, in Nairobi from 10 to
13 February 1987. He also promised that
the Bank would:

- **design action plans in selected countries
  so that agricultural, industrial,
  educational and health programmes
  promote women's progress along with
  other development goals;**
- **emphasise issues affecting women in**

dialogues with member countries;
- **encourage development policies that provide
  adequate incentives for women and ensure that
  they have the means to respond;**
- **develop programme initiatives in agricultural
  extension and agricultural credit targeted for
  women, and expand credit and training for
  women to improve their employment prospects in
  other sectors;**
- **promote formal and informal education for
  women and girls.**

In April 1987 the World Bank issued
*Protecting the Poor during Periods of
Adjustment.* Originally prepared for the

IMF/WB Development Committee, to serve as the basis for their discussion of the impact of adjustment measures on the poor and of how adjustment policies might be supplemented or modified to protect the poor, it has much in common with *Adjustment with a Human Face*. Both accept the need for adjustment, for targeting the poor and vulnerable, and for extreme economy if realistic programmes are to be prepared and implemented at a time of severe constraints.

The Bank paper essentially concentrates on how to add compensatory measures focused on the poor to existing adjustment programmes, which it is at pains to protect from any disruption; it neither recognises nor explores the extent to which the unqualified promotion of free market policies may conflict with the targeting and deliberate interference with the market needed to support employment, the informal sector, and protection of vulnerable groups. In contrast, the UNICEF report calls for more expansionary *macro* policies and underlines the need for restructuring policies in the productive and social sectors, as well as the need for *meso* policies to help direct more attention and resources to poor and vulnerable groups in general.

The reaction of non-governmental organisations to the World Bank paper was one of disappointment that poverty was treated as a supplementary consideration, and that the paper allowed little scope for changing the design of adjustment programmes. It was felt that programmes which concentrate on human capital development and on agrarian reform could be efficient instruments of growth and effective with respect to equity, and that measures geared to increasing efficiency need not have a high social cost. Nevertheless, it was accepted that equity might have some cost in terms of growth.

The World Bank has shown itself very receptive to these comments, and values its continued collaboration with the NGO community. Nevertheless, the verdict of a group of NGO activists, which organised a Permanent People's Tribunal at the time of the IMF/World Bank meeting in Berlin in September 1988, was extremely critical of the policies of the two institutions, whose structural adjustment policies

caused a growing net transfer of resources from indebted countries to creditor countries. Consequently ... living standards in indebted countries have deteriorated. The environment has been irreversibly damaged and living areas of indigenous peoples have been destroyed. The payment of reparations should therefore be considered.

In a statement to the UN Economic and Social Council in July 1988, the World Bank insisted that:

The question is whether there are ways in which the adjustment process can be designed and complemented to minimise the difficulties experienced by low-income and deprived groups, such as women. Two areas offer the greatest scope for doing this: ensuring that social expenditures, such as those in health and education, are cost effective and focussed on the poor; and compensating the poor directly.

The statement made it clear that the World Bank had become an increasingly sensitive advocate of the importance of women's concerns in the developing world and the development process, and had identified this as a priority area for increased attention. Pointing out that women represent 50% of the adult world population and one-third of the official labour force, perform nearly two-thirds of all working hours for which they receive only one-third of world income, and own less than 1% of world property, the statement surmised that 'development cannot advance far if women are left significantly behind.'

Since UNICEF first drew attention in 1987 to the need for 'adjustment with a human face' international recognition of the social effects of economic adjustment policies has been gaining ground. Michel Camdessus, Managing Director of the International Monetary Fund, expressed two convictions when issuing a recent IMF review of the impact on the poorest groups of Fund-supported programmes:

The first is that adjustment does not have to lower basic human standards. In this context, the efforts of fellow agencies of the UN family both to protect social programmes in the face of unavoidable budget cuts and to make some programmes more efficient – delivering better services at less cost – exemplify the types of things that are essential. My second conviction is that the more adjustment efforts give proper weight to social realities – especially the implications for the poorest – the more successful they are likely to be.

He continued to state the case bluntly:

People know something about how to ensure that the very poor are spared by the adjustment effort. In financial terms, it might not cost very much. Why? Because if you look at the share of the poorest groups in the distribution of these countries' income, it is a trifling amount. Thus, to maintain their share of global income during an adjustment period, or even increase it, need not cost much, contrary to what people say. The World Bank has published social indicators of development for a long list of developing countries which show the

share of the poverty groups in national income. You will see that the poorest 40% of the population in many cases receives only 10% or less of total income. This 10% level can be maintained or even increased by 10% – making it 11% for the poor – only if everyone else makes a slight sacrifice. Unfortunately, it is generally 'everyone else', and not the poverty groups, that is represented in government.[11]

DEBT **RELIEF, DEVELOPMENT AND PROTECTIONISM** ☐ At the present time (early 1990) major new moves are afoot for dealing with Third World debt. Already at the 1988 Toronto Summit major industrialised nations agreed in principle on a series of measures to reduce the debt burden for some of the most affected nations in sub-Saharan Africa. The consensus now emerging is that debt servicing must be reduced not only to the point where developing countries can cope with debt repayments, but to the point at which their economies can grow out of their indebtedness. As these measures take place, it will be essential to ensure that they are translated into benefits for the poorest groups in the countries concerned.

A second element is the necessity for commercial banks, holding some 60% of the developing world's debt, to accept a significant part of the losses involved in debt reduction. When lending policies turn out to have been unsound, then losses must be taken. And a third, and most important, element is that industrialised governments' role in tackling this crisis must be to assist in the promotion of growth in the developing world by significantly increasing flows of official development assistance. 'Without such (combined) action, today's adjustment policies[12] will amount to little more than a rearranging of the furniture inside the debtors' prison.'

The 1988 *Trade and Development Report* issued by the UN Conference on and Development (UNCTAD) predicted that a reduction of 30% in the commercial debts of the 15 most indebted developing countries would result in a 25% increase in their national incomes over the next five years, and that this would in turn lead to an increase in their demand for imports of some $18 billion a year – one-third of which would be spent on exports from the United States.

> A permanent reduction of interest payments... combined with debt relief and new financial flows in assistance to sub-Saharan African countries, would contribute to raising significantly developing country demand for US exports and thus to easing the trade imbalances among the industrialised countries.

A similar argument could also be applied to the economies of Europe and Japan. The UN Secretary-General's *Report on the External Debt Crisis and Development* suggested that the time was ripe to give serious consideration to specific debt-reduction schemes such as this.

The International Fund for Agricultural Development (IFAD) has also put forward a proposal on debt which could significantly alleviate this burden: to allow African countries with debt service ratios of more than 20% to repay a part of their bilateral official debts, not otherwise written off, in local currencies, to be used for financing development projects and programmes under agreed conditions. UNICEF has made a similar suggestion, that part of a country's debt in foreign currency could be forgiven by donor countries, or by commercial banks, in exchange for the establishment of a fund in local currency to be used by UNICEF or similar institutions, in collaboration with the government, for activities benefiting children and the poor.

UNICEF has also joined with Midland Bank (UK) in a debt-for-development swap in the Sudan. The Bank has donated

its entitlement to repayments of $800,000 for the financing of a health, water and reforestation programme in the Kordofan region. In the United States, three environmental organisations (the Sierra Club, American Farmland Trust and the Natural Resources Defense Council) are engaged in a cooperative effort with the African Development Bank in proposing ways to use debt relief for environmental purposes. Called the 'NGO Outreach Project', the partnership is designed to bring new economic and social resources to bear on the environmental problems of Africa.[13]

Another environmental organisation, the World Wide Fund for Nature (previously the World Wildlife Fund), has been involved in 'debt for nature' swaps in Ecuador, Costa Rica and the Philippines. A piece of each country's debt was bought at a discounted rate and returned to it through the WWF which put the money into conservation. In Ecuador, the President of the Fundación Natura suggested that WWF buy up to $10m of Ecuadorian debt from US banks. The face amount was converted through Ecuador's Central Bank into local currency bonds held by the Fundación Natura. Interest on the bonds is used to finance existing and new parklands, the training of personnel, and environmental education. When the bonds mature in nine years the money will become an endowment for the Fundación, and in the meantime the organisation has funds for day-to-day work and an assured income that lets it make some long-range plans.[14]

These imaginative plans have nevertheless been criticised by development experts as being a good deal for US banks but no gift for developing countries. An article in the *Los Angeles Times* has pointed out:

By donating unwanted debt, banks will

get to take a tax deduction equal to the dollar value of the local currency received by the US non-profit group. In addition, banks can claim a loss for the difference between the amount of the contribution and the value of the original loan... Yet what about the Third World? Granted, a foreign debt obligation converted into local money is easier to meet, but it is not cost-free. A central bank must either decide to run the presses and thereby pay indirectly through inflation, or it must divert resources from other national priorities, [which] heightens the role of US bankers as Third World policy-makers and development planners... As one official put it, 'How would you like it if the Japanese used your trade deficit to buy the Grand Canyon?'[15]

Meanwhile, President Barber Conable has stressed the World Bank's determination to play a central role in assisting heavily indebted nations. Addressing the UN Development Committee in 1988, he spoke of modifications in IBRD lending terms, and said that a reduction to zero of the commitment fee on credits approved by the International Development Association (IDA, the World Bank affiliate which lends on special terms to the poorest countries) would be considered. He suggested that IDA commitments would be about $4.2 billion by the end of 1988.

The Group of 24 developing countries has welcomed the agreement on a $74.8 billion World Bank general capital increase, and urged its quick ratification. They have also emphasised the urgent need for increased flows of concessional resources to low-income countries, and urged industrialised nations to meet this need through measures such as interest rate relief, further conversions of loans into grants, and outright loan cancellations.

Noting that in 1980 rich nations trans-ferred a net of $35 billion to poor nations, a bipartisan report to the then US Vice-President George Bush in December 1988 emphasised that there was now a $30 billion annual net transfer from poor to rich nations, and that after seven years the debt crisis had only become more threatening. Echoing the words of Kenneth Dadzie, Secretary-General of UNCTAD, it said that the real threat stems from the continuous postponement of development in the poorer countries; 'the longer the problem continues, the greater the chance one of the big Latin debtors will suffer a social, political or economic crisis.' Tom Wicker, in his report in the *New York Times*, concluded that 'a more accurate word would be "disaster", the consequences of which would surely be felt in the United States too.'[16] The debt problem is not confined to Latin America, of course; other heavily-indebted developing countries are vulnerable to social, political and/or economic crises, the consequences of which would be just as catastrophic for the industrialised countries.

Finally, on 10 March 1989 US Treasury Secretary Nicholas Brady pronounced the magic words 'debt reduction', as part of 'new thinking' on the part of the US Administration on the debt crisis, subsequent to the policy devised by previous Treasury Secretary (now Secretary of State) James Baker. Although the 'Brady Plan' only proposes 'voluntary' debt reduction by creditor banks, and expects debtor countries to retrieve private capital which has fled to safe hiding places in the North, it is an important switch in favour of debt relief and of committing public funds to the undertaking, and of allowing Japan to play a major role.

Subsequently, Michel Camdessus, managing director of the International Monetary Fund, announced on 20 March 1989 that the IMF could facilitate debt reduction by providing resources to allow

53

ECONOMIC TRENDS The chart shows what has happened to economic development in the major regions of the world during the 1980s

Gross domestic product per capita, by region of the world, 1980-86 (1980=100)

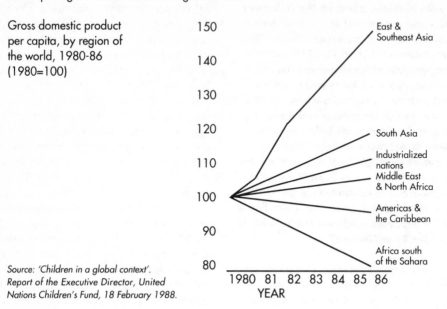

Source: 'Children in a global context'. Report of the Executive Director, United Nations Children's Fund, 18 February 1988.

WHERE AID GOES The chart shows how the total aid of the eighteen Western industri-alised countries is distributed among the richer and poorer developing countries.

OECD aid distribution by groups of developing countries at different income levels, 1985/86

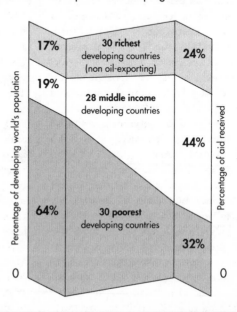

Source: OECD and World Bank.

a cash buyback of some Third World debts, to purchase collateral for an asset exchange, or to secure interest payments. He said, however, that it would be 'undesirable' for the IMF to extend guarantees for servicing the debt, and insisted that for debt reduction to be effective it was essential for debtor countries to pursue strong medium-term adjustment policies 'to ensure that freed-up resources are productively invested'.[17] (According to *The Economist*, 'good' debtors would receive IMF loans even if there were no final commitments to an overall loan programme from banks and other creditors; all the Fund would require would be 'a reasonable expectation that these will shortly be forthcoming'. The Fund would also help a country replenish its reserves used up in buying back its debt.[18])

M. Camdessus also indicated that industrialised countries could do more to help debtor countries by keeping interest rates low, pointing out that the 15 biggest debtors alone paid $10 billion more in interest in the past year. He also stressed the essential need for a restructuring of world trading patterns:

Let us not lose sight of the contribution that industrial country governments could make to the recovery prospects of the indebted countries by progressively dismantling barriers to international trade and by adopting a more balanced mix of anti-inflationary financial policies.[19]

Under the Brady Plan, approved by the International Monetary Fund's policy-making Interim Committee on 4 April 1989, the IMF and the World Bank would cooperate more closely in channelling debt reduction aid to countries willing to accept economic adjustment programmes. Japan has reiterated an offer of additional finance – some $4.5 billion over three years – in parallel to Fund arrangements, and the Fund and Bank have been instructed to set aside for debt reduction operations a portion of their lending to countries undertaking sound economic reforms, on the assumption that this would be accompanied by new money from the banks.

Some members of the Interim Committee warned against transforming the bad debts of commercial banks into bad debts of international institutions, and argued against interest support. 'Ironically', said *The Economist*, 'the interim committee devoted little time to two landmines that lie in the way of the debtors' eventual recovery: the American budget deficit that keeps interest rates high, and growing American protectionism that threatens their exports.'[20]

On 28 January 1990 the representatives of some 450 foreign banks signed an agreement to lighten Mexico's debt burden – the first success of the Brady Plan in political terms, though not perhaps in economic terms. 'The agreement will indeed reduce Mexico's debt to the banks. But [the] central issue is financing the country's growth – finding the capital to build modern industry... even with this agreement Mexico will continue to have a large trade deficit that has to be balanced by foreign investment', commented the *Washington Post*. 'That is where the Brady plan's weakness lies. It gives banks incentives to reduce debt, but when banks are reducing old debts to a customer they get very reluctant to offer new loans. It is fair to say that this agreement will give Mexico relief in one part of its international account but will make it harder to finance the remainder.'[21] Meanwhile, the *International Herald Tribune*, 12 February, reported that poor people in Brazil had started looting food stores as Brazil's monthly inflation rate soared.[22]

The Brady Plan is a step forward, but

in the view of many it does not go far enough. It makes the (dubious?) assumption that 'capital flight' can be reversed, and does not query the thrust of IMF structural adjustment programmes. There is an urgent need also for those programmes to be 'adjusted' so that the heaviest burdens do not fall upon the poor and the social services, and to reinstate net North-South financial flows through improved global economic conditions. It is clear that the shape and design of structural adjustment policies, and of international trading arrangements, must change if development is not to stall completely, and if women's essential role in social and economic progress is to be fully recognised.

As the ILO working paper for its High-Level Meeting on Employment and Structural Adjustment points out, a first requirement is a greater recognition by all countries of the interdependence of national economies, and what that implies:

A major responsibility for improving the functioning of the international trade, payments and financial system lies with the industrialised countries which need to coordinate their macro-economic, fiscal and financial policies in order to overcome their balance of payments imbalances, reduce interest rate and stabilise exchange rates. They need to aim at non-inflationary growth, and to take special steps to improve employment opportunities for their own people.

Protectionism is an inefficient and ineffective way of promoting growth and employment... any benefits gained are more than outweighed by lost opportunities – i.e. the jobs that could be created through an expansion of world trade. Protectionism by one country only delays adjustment, and passes the burden of adjustment on to other countries. Governments, employers' organisations and trade unions in industrialised countries need to educate the public and their members on the dangers of protectionism, while at the same time making every

effort to assist workers and enterprises in adjusting constructively to greater international competition.[23]

Referring on 7 March 1989 to a document on Protectionism and Structural Adjustment submitted to the 131-member Trade and Development Board at its spring session in Geneva, the UNCTAD Secretary-General said that 'neither economic growth nor the commitments renewed in launching the Uruguay Round have broken the back of protectionism in the developed countries.' On the contrary, he noted, 'non-tariff measures have been renewed and new ones introduced. Export subsidies, 'voluntary' export restraints and surveillance measures are on the increase; so is the use of anti-dumping laws for protectionist purposes.' Imports from developing countries were often the specific targets of such measures and in any case suffered from them. While there had been 'a widespread though varied movement towards trade-oriented reform in developing countries', such measures in themselves could not succeed 'without a supportive combination of financial and technological inflows and export expansion.' Positive structural adjustments were required in the major markets for developing countries' products, 'induced by deliberate government policies as well as by market forces.'[24]

In a report released in Geneva at the end of March 1989, ILO called for a global effort to overcome the debt problem and 'disarray' in international economic cooperation, one 'perverse' consequence of which is that poor countries have become net exporters of capital. Pointing to ways in which to 'redress the dangerous imbalances in the world economy while reinforcing the adjustment policies incumbent upon all countries', and advocating the solidarity of the industrialised North in aiding the South, it urged greater efficiency on the part of the latter in the use of resources and a reversal of the effects of past short-term stabilisation measures, which have provoked greater poverty and thereby diminished capacity for growth precisely when it was most needed. It should be possible, said the report, through a judicious use of macro- and micro-economic policies, through institutional reforms in the economic sphere, and through greater budgetary and monetary discipline, for developing countries to extricate themselves from the crisis that still engulfs so many of them.[25]

THE KHARTOUM DECLARATION □

The Economic Commission for Africa's Conference of Ministers, meeting in Niamey, Niger, from 14 to 17 April 1988, endorsed the Khartoum Declaration adopted by the international conference organised, as a collective UN inter-agency effort, in Khartoum from 5 to 8 March 1988. The objectives were to critically assess the central role that the human dimension plays in Africa's efforts towards achieving economic recovery and accelerated self-sustained and self-reliant development, and to propose practical measures through which the strengthening and further development of human capacities, and enhancement of conditions of human well-being, are made integral parts of national strategies, plans and programmes of socio-economic recovery and development.

Affirming that the human dimension is the *sine qua non* of economic recovery, the Declaration asserts that there can be no real structural adjustment or economic recovery in the absence of the human imperative, meaning that the vulnerable and impoverished, the uprooted and ravaged, poor women, children and youth, the disabled, the aged, the rural and urban poor – every group and individual in society which is in some way disadvantaged –

must be given paramount consideration in the socio-economic development process.

A paper prepared for the conference by the African Training and Research Centre for Women pointed out that all aspects of the crisis have had an impact on women in terms of income, productivity, health, employment and the general well-being of women and their families:

The relevant questions here are whether women are suffering more than men, and why. If that is the case, what can be done to alleviate women's plight? In what capacity are women being involved in the development process? How could they be involved to increase productivity? As part of human resources, to what extent is women's potential being developed, identified and appropriately utilised?[26]

The paper stresses that awareness of the real extent of women's economic activity, the importance of women's income, and the contribution of women to national development is essential to the formulation of adequate policy measures and the adjustment of strategies in such a way as to benefit both women and men in the area of employment and, in turn, to enhance the development process as a whole. It suggests that governments should give serious attention to the implementation of recommendations such as those made in the 'Kilimanjaro Programme of Action for African Population and Self-Reliant Development', adopted at a conference organised by the UN Economic Commission for Africa in Arusha, Tanzania, in 1984, to the effect that governments should:

- **introduce programmes designed to reduce the heavy burden on rural women, including labour-saving technology in agriculture, industry and domestic work;**
- **recognise the importance and changing role of women as mothers and workers in all sectors of**

the economy; and
* **ensure that rural populations have easy access to modern agricultural technology and equal opportunities to use credit and other resource-generating facilities.**[27]

Supporting the role of non-governmental organisations in contributing to Africa's recovery, the Khartoum Declaration asks governments to give due recognition to African NGOs, create the legal and fiscal framework for their activities, and encourage them to respond to the human and social needs of the poor, especially in rural areas where structural adjustment programmes have resulted in the reduction of social services. It also suggests that NGOs have an important role at the international level in monitoring the implementation of international commitments and improving public awareness of the realities of African countries and societies.

Pointing to the 'shared partnership' implied by the UN Programme of Action for African Economic Recovery and Development, 1986–90, the Declaration insists that Africa's efforts must be matched by the international community:

'Alas, the international community has not yet fulfilled its part of the bargain. African economic recovery continues to be threatened on every front by catastrophic debt, collapsed commodity prices, stagnating concessional flows and crippling terms of trade. Because the front-line of recovery is the human dimension, the human dimension is at greatest risk. If structural adjustment with a human face does not succeed, then the failure, in considerable measure, will be laid at the feet of the international community.'

THE WORLD SURVEY ON THE ROLE OF WOMEN IN DEVELOPMENT □

The UN Division for the Advancement of Women, in Chapter 2 of its Update of the World Survey, suggests that there is a general international consensus that adjustment policies should be determined with full consideration of their effects on *people*. How this can be done with regard to the advancement of women will require studies of national experience in this area. Among approaches to examine would be:

* **differential policies for rural and urban areas, including analysis of the effects of changes in subsidy or price control structures for essential goods;**
* **policies tailored to sectors in which women have significant participation;**
* **encouragement of women to enter sectors promoted by adjustment, and monitoring their status in these sectors;**
* **monitoring of policies to ensure that they do not have disproportionately negative effects upon the poor;**
* **trade-offs between spending-reduction policies and compensatory programmes such as nutritional programmes;**
* **protection of programmes, such as education and training, which develop human capital and help promote equality;**
* **encouragement of sectors, such as food production and small-scale manufacturing, which already have significant participation by women;**
* **at the international level, a better balance between adjustment and financing, including debt rescheduling and cancellation and interest-rate concessions.**

At its 29 March – 7 April 1989 Session in Vienna, the UN Commission on the Status of Women was told by the Director-General of the United Nations Office in Vienna that evidence was mounting that *progress towards the full economic and political participation of women was slowing or had actually stopped.*

Among the resolutions adopted at the

session was one relating to the question of women's unpaid work and activities in the informal sector. It invited UN agencies to give priority to the collection of information on women's participation in the informal and unpaid sectors of the economy of member states, and recommended that the report on statistics and indicators scheduled for submission to the Commission on the Status of Women at its 35th session should include suggestions for the determination of methods of including into the gross national product the economic value of work carried out by women in the informal sectors by using, *inter alia*, the work done by UN specialised agencies such as INSTRAW.

1   Nairobi: 'Forward-Looking Strategies for the Advancement of Women', paragraph 96.
2   Ibid, paragraph 97.
3   *Adjustment with a Human Face*, UNICEF, 1987, Oxford University Press.
4   The term *meso* (middle) has been chosen to designate policies at an intermediate level between *micro* and *macro*.
5   UNICEF, op.cit.
6   Frances Stewart, 'Supporting Productive Employment among Vulnerable Groups', UNICEF, op. cit.
7   Per Pinstrup Andersen, 'Nutrition Interventions,' UNICEF, op.cit.
8   UNICEF Annual Report, Uruguay, 1987.
9   'Progress Report on Achievements made in the Implementation of UNICEF Policy on Women in Development', E/ICEF/1988/L.1. *Also*: Supplement No. 8, Official Records 1988.
10 Frances Stewart, 'Monitoring and Statistics for Adjustment with a Human Face.' UNICEF, op.cit.
11 As reported in *The State of the World's Children, 1989*, UNICEF, New York.
12 Ibid, p.23.
13 *Go-Between*, newsletter published by the UN Non-Governmental Liaison Service, Geneva.
14 UN *Development Forum*, Jan/Feb. 1989.
15 Patti Petesch, *Los Angeles Times*, 9 December 1987.
16 *International Herald Tribune*, 6 December 1988.
17 Reported by Carl Gewirtz in the *International Herald Tribune*, 21 March 1989.
18 *The Economist*, 25 March 1989.
19 *International Herald Tribune*, 27 March 1989.
20 'Debt relief: the Brady plan's Foggy Bottom', *The Economist*, London, 8 April 1989.
21 Editorial page of the *International Herald Tribune*, 7 March 1990.
22 James Brooke, New York Times Service, in the IHT, 12 February 1990.
23 Working document for High-Level Meeting on Employment and Structural Adjustment, ILO, Geneva 23–25 November 1987. WEP 2–46–04–03 (Doc.1).
24 As reported in press release TAD/INF/2000, 7 March 1989, UNCTAD, Geneva.
25 Report of the Director-General to the International Labour Conference, Geneva 7–28 June 1989, *Recovery and Employment*, as reported by UN Information Service, April 1989.
26 *The Impact of the Economic Crisis on the vulnerable groups in African societies: Women*. ATRCW, UN Economic Commission for Africa, Addis Ababa, 1988
27 Ibid.

PROPOSALS BY NON-GOVERNMENTAL ORGANISATIONS

Who are the poor? Development Non-Governmental Organisations (NGOs) are deeply concerned about the unprecedented scale of the crisis. Commenting upon World Bank proposals, they have drawn attention to the fact that 'the poor' are not a homogeneous group – some are very much poorer than others. For example, female-headed families comprise about one-third of rural households and these rarely have access either to credit or to the labour inputs required to increase production. Given that increased rural wealth is likely to lead to higher prices of land, fertilisers and even household supplies, relative poverty usually, in time, becomes absolute poverty.

NGOs INSIST THAT EXTERNAL FACTORS be more fully considered, in particular the need for 'structural adjustment' in the North and the hostile environment which besets primary commodity producers. More attention should be given to the dynamics of reform, and there should be a change in the 'ground rules' of adjustment. Rather than 'subsidised credit' to the poor, their access to credit on fair terms should be guaranteed.

At a meeting of NGOs in Vienna during the 19 March to 7 April 1989 session of the UN Commission on the Status of Women, the representative of the International Federation of University Women pointed out that the dependence of national economies on international economic conditions meant that, when examining the economic role of women and means to achieve equality, it was necessary to examine international economic issues. The debt crisis had been a major factor in the persistence of economic stagnation for developing countries, and its solution was a key development issue. Adjustment today must deal with the question of the role of the poor as a vital productive resource with the potential to contribute more to economic recovery and growth.[1]

Participants in a special symposium on 'Women's Voice in the North-South Dialogue' drew up a 'Barcelona Declaration' for presentation to the European Conference of Parliamentarians and NGOs on North-South Interdependence and Solidarity, held in Madrid, 1–3 June 1988, which *inter alia* proposed the following:

1. **Women should be recognised as agents of development, and all kinds of work that they provide, visible or hidden, should be taken into account by economic research, by national accounting agencies and in planning.**

2. **Within scrutiny of the debt problem, priority should be given to the interests of the poor, notably poor women, to investment in the social sector, to protection of the environment and to the strengthening of democratic institutions. For the poorest countries, the debt should be cancelled and the finance recouped thereby used for a special fund directed towards jobs for women, the creation of services, and environmental protection.**

3. **Programmes of development cooperation concerning agriculture should stress the basic role of women as food producers, and lay emphasis on access to education, property rights, and financial credits.**

4. Women should be present, on an equal footing with men, at all national and international fora, governmental or non-governmental, where decisions are taken which have economic consequences. Positive measures should be taken to ensure that the objectives of the United Nations Decade for Women concerning development be reached by the year 2000.[2]

And at a conference in The Netherlands on 'Women and the Debt Crisis', 8 March 1988, Anne-Marie Beulink (member of The Netherlands Organisation for International Development (NOVIB) and of the World Bank/NGO Committee) pointed out that the various proposals for overcoming the debt problem were still based on the assumption that the poor countries have the obligation to repay the loans.

Debts may be cancelled, converted, written off or whatever, but these are only *ad hoc* measures. Needed is a guarantee that no new debt crisis will emerge in another ten years or so, and this can only be given when the international monetary, financial and economic system is fundamentally changed... the debt crisis is only the tip of an iceberg: it rests on a much vaster system of economic and political inequality in the world.

If we realise that, it should also be obvious that the debt crisis can only be solved by a development model in which the equal standing of all countries and, especially, the equality of all people, men and women alike, is the dominant and decisive characteristic... the say of women should finally become reality or everything will just be a futile exercise with a very low credibility rating.

In her recommendations to women, Ms Beulink suggested that they should acquire more knowledge of, and insight into, national and international economic policies, so as to make the connection between them and women's interests. 'Our first priority is for women to arrive at the conviction that economic and monetary and financial affairs are not the sole concern of men, but... have a vital bearing on our own lives as well.'[3]

RELIGIOUS ORGANISATIONS ☐ Already in December 1986 the Pontifical Commission's *Iusticia et Pax* suggested that:

The debt of developing countries must be placed in a broader context of economic, political and technological relations which point to the increased interdependence between countries, as well as to the need for international collaboration in pursuing the objectives of the common good. In order to be just, this interdependence should give rise to new and broader expressions of solidarity which respect the equal dignity of all peoples, rather than lead to domination by the strongest, to national egoism, to inequalities and injustices... Solidarity implies an awareness and acceptance of co-responsibility for the causes and the solutions relative to international debt... In order to emerge from the international debt crisis, the various partners must agree on an equitable sharing of the adjustment efforts and the necessary sacrifices, taking into account the priority to be given to the needs of the most deprived peoples.

The statement goes on to say that, due to their greater economic power, the industrialised countries bear a heavier responsibility which they must acknowledge and accept, even if the economic crisis has often challenged them with grave problems of reconversion and employment. 'The time is over when they can act without regard for the effects of their own policies on other countries... In particular, has the time not come for the industrialised countries to draw up a broad plan of cooperation and assistance for the good of the developing countries?

Without drawing a parallel with what was done after World War II to accelerate the reconstruction and economic recovery of countries seriously damaged during that conflict, is it not imperative to start working on a new system of aid from the industrialised countries to the less prosperous ones, in the interests of all and especially because it would mean restoring hope to suffering populations? Such a contribution... would seem indispensable in order to enable the developing countries to launch and conclude successfully, in cooperation with the industrialised countries and the international organisations, the long-term programmes they need to undertake as soon as possible.

In a Position Paper published in early 1988, CIDSE (International Cooperation for Development and Solidarity), which brings together 14 Catholic development organisations located in Europe and North America, considered that the international debt crisis was intensifying rather than diminishing; the mountain of debt was growing, with extensions of credit being largely for servicing of existing debt rather than new investment. In a critical appraisal of current policies, the Position Paper considered the following major themes:

- **the legitimacy of debt**
- **the responsibility of the North**
- **internal problems, their impact on women, alternative solutions**
- **NGO proposals for a reasonable debt strategy and campaigning**
- **practical responses by grassroots NGOs**

Among proposals for new approaches, the Position Paper listed the following: rescheduling, conversions to grants and moratoria on repayments, debt capping, debt-equity swaps, debt-conservation swaps, debt-development swaps, own debt purchase, and repudiation. Of these, no single one was considered adequate to meet the needs of all cases of debtor and creditor countries.[4]

Private banks must accept co-responsibility for the crisis, given that their lending practices were a major cause, says the paper. And if projects financed by the World Bank are to have a positive impact, governments of the South must clearly determine their priorities so that the World Bank can integrate those priorities into its policies. Two objectives should be paramount: the direct struggle against poverty (labour-intensive projects in rural or urban areas, social infrastructure benefiting the poorest, etc.) and the overall reinforcement of development potential through the development of renewable energy sources, agricultural research adapted to local conditions, combatting the over-exploitation of natural resources, etc.

The CIDSE paper considered that OECD countries should clearly demonstrate their political will to create a climate favourable to economic recovery by (i) appropriate measures to stimulate investment, (ii) better policy co-ordination, (iii) formulating and effectively applying measures to control interest rates and to effect the return to a stable international monetary system, and (iv) ensuring that multilateral institutions play a full role in the promotion of development. However, it was equally indispensable that governments of the South implement policies which would involve *the population as a whole* in the revitalisation of the development process. Public spending reductions should be applied to arms and other luxury purchases and to 'prestige' projects, and, where cuts in social services were necessary, the weakest and most vulnerable groups should be insulated from their effects. There should be better distribution of income, an attack on corruption and capital flight, and more just taxation at higher income levels.

Non-governmental organisations should support the so-called informal sector, which in many Third World countries represents between 40% and 60% of the productive age labour force, including improvement of productive capacity through appropriate training; assistance for purchase of raw materials; support in marketing of goods to meet local needs; training and advice regarding organisation, administration and management; and extending access to credit.

> Finally, CIDSE listed the following questions in an appeal to the political will, to the foresight and to the imagination of all the actors concerned, North and South alike:
>
> • How can we avoid repeating the mistakes in economic and financial management which have been made over the last decade and which have led to the present situation?
> • How can we ensure that the new policies and new instruments to be adopted lead to more equitable relations between nations?
> • How can we ensure that all measures to stabilise the international financial system are not taken at the expense of the lowest income groups in the debtor countries?[5]

An Ecumenical Hearing on 'The International Monetary System and the Churches' Responsibility' took place in Berlin in August 1988 prior to the Annual Meeting there of the IMF and World Bank. It was organised by more than 20 West German church action groups in cooperation with the World Council of Churches and the Lutheran World Federation, and was attended by top offi-cials from the international financial institutions, who shared the 'witness stand' with representatives of grass-roots organisations from the South.

Witnesses from Africa, Asia, Latin America and the Caribbean gave powerful testimony on the human costs of indebtedness and found hope in the emergence of people's self-help organisations. World Bank and IMF representatives conceded that poor countries must operate in a global economy now threatened by rising protectionism and the prospect of a recession, and acknowledged that the policies they prescribe have, at least in some instances, negatively affected vulnerable social groups.

Various experiences and action models for dealing with the debt problem were discussed, including the formation of broad-based coalitions to press governments and commercial banks for change and proposals for rechannelling church resources, such as the Ecumenical Development Cooperative Society (EDCS), in support of alternative approaches in banking and development.[6]

The impossibility of overcoming the Third World debt crisis through 'technical' solutions is underlined in the recent survey by Tamara Kunanayakam published in the November 1988 issue of LWF's *World Development Education Forum*. These 'shift the burden of debt to Third World countries which in turn transfer the staggering costs of debt repayment to the poorest and weakest sections of their populations':

A durable solution that would preclude a repetition of the debt crisis should address the real economic aspects of the present world order, as well as unjust social structures in the Third World that create and maintain poverty and oppression for the majority of their peoples. The political challenge has been

sidestepped by focussing exclusively on monetary solutions: crisis management is only a means of postponing the debt problem in the interest of the creditors, and is therefore an inappropriate instrument for achieving long-term structural changes...

A political solution is moreover an urgent necessity 'as debt servicing and adjustment programmes pose an enormous threat to political stability in the debtor Third World nations, and to world peace... [This] has become a national security problem for the United States,' continues Ms Kunanayakam, referring to a recent study by the Debt Crisis Network, which commented that:

If political instability in the Southern Hemisphere is a major threat to US national security, then the debt crisis and the failure of development, not East–West conflict, is the major culprit. As poverty and popular unrest in the Third World grow, peace everywhere is placed in danger'... The debt crisis – and current IMF policies supposedly aimed at its alleviation – have also eroded the economic stability of developed countries' economies and banking systems. In turn, it has affected not only Third World but also US farmers, business, workers, taxpayers and the poor.'

THE UN/NGO WORKSHOP IN OXFORD □ At an important UN/NGO Workshop held in Oxford in September 1987,[9] participants considered that stabilisation and adjustment policies implemented thus far had exacerbated the problem by focusing solely upon restoring 'external balance' and increasing the Third World's capacity to repay debt, rather than creating the foundations for development. An alternative adjustment policy that responds to the needs of the

poor and promotes development would require significant political will and the organisation and participation in the decision-making process of the poor themselves, particularly women. It was essential that NGOs support the people's efforts to survive the crisis, give voice to the needs and aspirations of the poor at national and international levels, respect, defend and promote people's own capacities and culture, build new institutions that respond to everyday struggles, and foster justice and solidarity.

At the international level, participants proposed that shareholders of banks and Northern governments should share the burden of a selective and progressive write-off of a portion of the debts and of lowering interest charges, and accept that a significant portion of the Third World debt simply cannot be repaid. In the case of the poorest, IDA-eligible countries, Northern governments should write off bilateral debts by converting them into grants. Protectionist measures should be condemned, and Northern aid should match the severity of the crisis. The adjustment process should be monitored. (See Chapter 11 for Workshop proposals concerning development education and action at national and local levels.)

---

1 Trijntje Faber, representative of the International Federation of University Women in the Netherlands.
2 Symposium held in Barcelona, 30–31 May 1988. European Conference of Parliamentarians and NGOs on North-South Interdependence and Solidarity, Council of Europe.
3 Anne-Marie Beulink, *Women and the Debt Crisis*, The Netherlands, 1988.
4 Explanations of these terms are included in Annexe 1.
5 CIDSE, *Third World Debt*. A Position Paper published in 1988, 1st Quarter, by International Cooperation for Development and Solidarity (CIDSE), 1-2 Ave.des Arts, Bte.6, 1040 Brussels.
6 Lynne Jones, 'What it Really Costs', *One World*, World Council of Churches, 150 route de Ferney, 1211 Geneva 20.
7 *From Debt to Development: Alternatives to the International Debt Crisis*. The Debt Crisis Network, Washington D.C.
8 Tamara Kunanayakam, 'The Debt Crisis and Development Disaster', *Development Education Forum*,

November 1988. Lutheran World Federation, 1211 Geneva 20.

9 UN/NGO Workshop on **Debt, Adjustment and the Needs of the Poor**, co-organised by UN Non-Governmental Liaison Service, OXFAM, at Queen Elizabeth House, Oxford, 19–22 September 1987.

5 RESPONSES AT THE GRASS-ROOTS

Developing countries face the greatest challenge. We must continue to take appropriate measures to equip women to attain their rightful place in the development process. To do otherwise amounts to a failure to utilise to the fullest a vital resource which could give a new impetus to our development efforts.

DAME NITA BARROW[1]

INTERNATIONAL AND GOVERNMENT POLICIES and 'human face' strategies are only part of the response to the world economic crisis. Of primary and growing importance are the 'self-reliance' strategies which are being initiated by community groups themselves in an effort to cope with the local effects of the world economic crisis. Among the most effective of these have been the women's groups which have formed in Latin America, Asia and Africa.

Anita Anand, Coordinator of Women, Communication and Development at IPS, the Third World news agency, has pointed out in *Development Forum* that the United Nations Decade for Women has enabled women to come out of their homes, organise with other women, establish their non-formal sector work into viable economic ventures, obtain loans, earn incomes, support their families, become more independent and participate in a world broader than their homes:

Bringing together people at the grassroots level as well as serving as intermediaries, non-governmental groups have organised credit schemes for the self-employed, small farmers and entrepreneurs, whom the macro-development projects cannot handle... The success stories of the decade are the micro-efforts... forcing governments and institutions to pay attention to those whose interests are easily forgotten, be they the poor, the minorities or women. Women have become organised at an unprecedented rate and have established networks within countries and regions, communicating their efforts with each other.[2]

Women in Jamaica are trying to deal with the effects of the economic crisis by becoming 'street higglers' (see Chapter 10). In Dominica the Southern Women's Organisation for Rural Development (SWORD) runs a sewing cooperative with two paid staff and a day-care centre, while Banana Bunch sells products made from surplus fruit. There are female farm and dairy co-ops in El Salvador. Poor and middle-class women in Chile have formed *Mujeres por la Vida* to protest against conditions in that country.[3]

The women of the Vera Cruz region of eastern Mexico, a dry, inhospitable cattle-raising area where poverty and malnutrition go hand in hand, fetch water and firewood at great distances from home, mill food grains and work as agricultural labourers. Sixty per cent of them are illiterate, and the area has a high mortality rate due to tuberculosis and respiratory and parasitic infections. Despite these conditions and a heavy domestic workload, the women requested training for income-producing activities, and several UN agencies, including the UN Fund for Women, and an international NGO, Zonta, have supported a project to provide time-saving technologies, a revolving loan fund, and training in agriculture and animal husbandry. The women are trained in maintenance and repair of equipment, and the project helps to increase their

A VOICE FROM THE SOUTH

I think the most unfortunate thing about the timing of the structural adjustment programmes in Africa is that it coincided with the period when we had built up a lot of hope for African women, especially immediately following the Decade for Women. When you look at the Forward Looking Strategies and the things that we as African women sought to do to improve or to advance ourselves, we see women are perhaps among the hardest hit by structural adjustment.

The Forward Looking Strategies talked a lot about food production, which in fact we have made the focus of our activities for this year and next year. We have been talking about improving resources to women's development programmes in areas such as education and extension. While our governments are cutting back on staffing expenditures, we are asking for more people to be employed so they can reach women farmers. We are asking for technology to ease the burden of African women.

Our colleague from Ghana has talked about women's education. This is an area in which we built a lot of hope, since more and more of our governments were allowing free education, especially at the basic level. We now see in many of our countries a reversion into the previous situation, where a family given the choice to send a girl or boy to school will opt to send a boy. It's frightening to think about what is going to happen to women – the growing illiteracy when we have set goals for eradicating female illiteracy by the year 2000. We see ourselves in a situation where many of our programmes were looking to get government subsidies and support to expand initiatives that we had started as NGOs, especially as part of our Decade for Women initiatives.

And now we find that governments aren't able to support or to supplement our efforts. In the area of health particularly, many NGOs, particularly women's NGOs, have gone into programmes for primary health care, for family planning, for training women at the community level to provide more and more education and to provide services. And health is one sector where most of our governments are now calling for cost sharings. It means now that a woman going to a clinic for family planning, which we have spent years motivating, which we have said is essential for higher advancement, may not be able to afford the fees. Communities are now leaning even more heavily than ever on women to provide services like water and day-care, when these were areas where women were going to get support so they could be relieved of their burdens of carrying community responsibility and become more productive.

Njoki Wainaina (Women's Task Force, Kenya)
at a meeting of the Liaison Committee
of Development NGOS to the European
Communities on 'Women and Debt'.
Brussels, 18–21 April 1989

involvement in local decision-making.[4]

Women's cooperatives in rural Senegal have been assisted by the UN Development Programme and the UN Capital Development Fund to ease the workload of 53,500 women through food processing technologies, while several non-governmental organisations have joined together to build village wells. Women's groups in Indonesia produce clothing, batik, woven articles, palm sugar, plaited bamboo products, roof tiles, silk fabric and embroidery with assistance from UNDP and the government of The Netherlands. In Laos, the Lao Women's Union is developing a textile industry in a new centre which has provided organised training for more than 140 women in spinning, dyeing, pre-weaving, garment-making, marketing, training and management activities. Assisted by UNDP, UNCDF, UNIFEM and the ILO, the centre employs 53 people, of whom 40 are women, and women hold all the key positions.[5]

Mothers Clubs, a traditional community organisation for women in Bolivia, undertake various activities aimed at improving the health status of mothers and their families. In one project assisted by the World Food Programme, food aid is used to help indigenous women in the Andean highlands increase their Clubs' income. WFP food rations are sold by the Clubs to their members for about half their market value. The funds generated from the sales are in turn used to support Club activities such as dressmaking, agricultural and small livestock activities, and to invest in laundries, bakeries, greenhouses and other small businesses. There are about 240 clubs with up to 100 members each, and so far about $1.5 million has been generated through the project.[6]

'In Bolivia, faced with the daily crisis of survival, women in the shanty towns organise communal kitchens to save cooking costs and to support destitute neighbours,' says Helen Allison, of War on Want in the UK:

Women's organisations, such as the Housewives Committees, have been vocal and often militant in their protests about the social costs of their country's debts... In March 1985 a hundred members of the Housewives Committee in La Paz went on a hunger strike. They were demanding that the government open 'popular stores' where the poorest people could buy the basic necessities – milk, rice, soap, kerosene – at fixed prices. With inflation at 5000% food prices were beyond reach, and hunger strike was the only option for Bolivian women. The strike lasted eleven days, ending when the government promised to control food prices.

Dr Chris Lewis of the University of Strathclyde, Scotland, writes in *Development Forum* about an interesting experiment carried out in the rural community of Injambakkam, in southern India, designed to assess the feasibility of self-reliant development through improved exploitation of local, indigenous resources – particularly bio-mass resources. It was undertaken in collaboration with the Murugappa Chettiar Research Centre (MCRC) of Madras, which would be responsible for manufacturing and installing the introduced technologies.

Initially the villagers showed little interest in the MCRC technologies, but relations thawed. One of the advantages of villager participation was that they could then explain to others why certain things were done – rather than preaching from an 'outsider'. One of the employed villagers actually wrote a book which, in the local dialect, explained the construction and benefits of a biogas plant, and received a small remuneration for his efforts.

'But perhaps MCRC's biggest coup,' reports Dr Lewis, 'was its ability to gain the interest of the village women who,

"Women grow around half of the world's food, but own hardly any land, find it difficult to get loans, and are overlooked by agricultural advisors and projects", says the State of the World's Women Report 1985.

Photo : Mike Abrahams/NETWORK

along with landless agricultural labourers, had the most to gain from technological improvements to reduce the daily drudgery of wood gathering or cooking for long hours.'

Adult education classes for women were organised in collaboration with the district Women's Voluntary **Services, initially much against the wishes of the *panchayat* president. They were taught about biogas plants, windmills, inland pisciculture, energy conservation, and the importance of indigenous participation in community development projects.**

70

Although opposition came from some of the men – particularly landed farmers wishing to maintain a status quo which was to their personal advantage, headmen from neighbouring villages began to take an active interest in what was happening in Injambakkam. Indeed, eight nearby villages pressed the MCRC to initiate similar programmes for their communities as well.[7]

The Jahaly Pacharr Smallholder (irrigated rice swamp) project, initiated in The Gambia in 1981, attempted to tackle the problems faced by women rice farmers. This meant, first, the provision of day-care centres for children of women whose workload increased due to the introduction of double cropping; and secondly, the upholding of their traditional cultivation rights. Under the new arrangements 95% of over 3,000 beneficiaries are women with credit and inputs provided directly to them. Over the period 1982–84 rice yields averaging six tonnes per hectare were achieved by women cultivators, compared with two and a quarter tonnes before the project.[8]

In Zanzibar a large-scale scheme to develop nearly 3,000 hectares of double-cropped irrigated rice land and 800 hectares of rain-fed rice land also recognises women's dominant role in the production of rice and other subsistence food crops. Both men and women are able to register as tenants, each being allocated one-tenth of a hectare of irrigated land or one-quarter of a hectare of rain-fed rice land.

The whole area was developed by the end of the second season in 1984, with women accounting for just over half the registered tenants and playing an active role in the scheme's tenants' association. Irrigation makes a new dry season crop possible and ensures reliable water supplies, so the grain available to the family and returns to labour have been increased. The tenants' association is also proving a means of increasing women's participation in village-level decision-making.

Evidence exists to show that the twin objectives of increasing national food supply and increasing the allocation of resources to women small farmers can be achieved with appropriate project and policy design. Agricultural policies have to avoid the misconception that women will automatically benefit if resources are targeted exclusively to the male head of household, says Richard Longhurst of the Institute of Development Studies (IDS), Sussex University.[9] (Or, indeed, that resources will not be better used if targeted directly towards women!)

UNIFEM REVOLVING LOAN FUNDS ☐

In Swaziland a revolving loan fund from the United Nations Development Fund for Women (UNIFEM) is assisting local women to be more economically independent by providing loans for means of production such as sewing machines; to help them in their businesses by providing loans for the purchase of raw materials at near factory prices; to support them in the provision of low-cost items which have a local market, such as school uniforms, thus assisting the economy of the rural development areas; and helping to train women in small-scale home industries so that they do not leave home in search of work. Only graduates of a skills training project (sewing, knitting, tie-dye, batik, welding, brick-making, leather work, cement water-jar construction) funded by the UN and the government of The Netherlands may apply for loans. Demand for credit is high. Repayment rate was 85% in 1986 and expected to rise to 90% with a default rate of about 2%.[10]

UNIFEM also provides 'coos' mills to The Gambia, to reduce the four to six hours a day women spend hand-pounding sorghum and millet. In five minutes these mills can grind as much grain as it takes five hours to pulverise by hand. Fuel-saving stoves in Burkina Faso consume 40–60% less firewood than the traditional 'three-stone' types and can be made locally. Chorkor fish-smokers, developed in Ghana and now used in Guinea, Togo, Guinea Bissau and Benin, can smoke ten times more fish than traditional smokers using the same amount of firewood.

The Ngusuria community of a Rift Valley Province, working with the Kenya Water for Health Organisation and various government departments, built a safe water system which eliminated the 14 kilometre walk which had previously taken women up to seven hours daily. It also provided power for a maize mill and water for a clinic, a cattle dip, demonstration farms for draught animals, new crops and reafforestation. Women gained time to attend courses in nutrition, adult education and literacy, and improved their health, hygiene and child-care practices. They also saved money previously spent on ground maize flour. Forestry programmes throughout Senegal, sponsored by a number of national and international NGOs, plant trees for fuelwood.[11]

SPECIAL BANKS FOR THE RURAL POOR □ In rural Bangladesh the credit needs of the landless are met by a unique project, the Grameen Bank, founded ten years ago by a young professor of economics at Chittagong University, Dr Mohammed Yunis. It has flourished in spite of having as its sole client the rural poor who, without collateral for their credit needs, had been bypassed by traditional banks which felt they could never repay their debts, and were thus at the mercy of moneylenders.

The Bank, with its special focus on women, has assisted the unemployed and underemployed to find gainful activity by undertaking income-generating activities, and soon gained the support of the Bangladesh Bank, nationalised commercial banks, and the International Fund for Agricultural Development, which provided a loan of $3.4 million. It now has 25% equity capital from government sources and 75% from the landless borrowers. According to a June 1986 report it operates 241 branches and encompasses about 171,000 members in 3,600 villages. Seventy per cent of its members are women.

Each branch is headed by a manager with a field staff of three men and three women, all of whom are required to live in the villages in which they work. Anybody who owns less than 0.5 acres of land or whose family assets do not exceed the value of one acre of cultivable land is eligible for a loan for income-generating activities, and women are especially encouraged to improve their household skills in order to produce goods and services in demand.

Loans have been used for a huge variety of activities in agriculture and forestry, livestock and fisheries, processing and manufacturing, trading and shopkeeping, and transport services. The bank has been particularly successful in creating new self-employment opportunities for women, who received 56% of the disbursements, and in achieving a very high pay-back rate – 99% on average, while the women have a 100% repayment rate.

Among the chief beneficiaries have been the textile weaving societies which produce hundreds of thousands of yards of silk saris and other products. A ready market exists for the products and services of the villagers, who only had to be provided money for rickshaws, handlooms, livestock and other capital goods. With capital, women buy paddy, process it and find a brisk market for it, particularly in the urban areas, instead of being employed daily at pittance rates by the grain merchants and moneylenders who formerly

The 12 + 12 Approach to Women

By Perdita Huston

FROM: INTERNATIONAL HERALD TRIBUNE, 23 JUNE 1988.

GENEVA — Each woman arrived wearing her best dress, with a baby on her back and carrying a worn plastic purse. The noonday meeting was held under the chief's tree. About 50 in all, the women sat together in the shade. They were visibly proud of what they had come to do.

The village was near Meri in northern Cameroon, a dry, unproductive region of an otherwise lush country. Three months before, each woman had borrowed $12 or so. Through a variety of creative activities — from cooking biscuits to be sold at market, to buying cloth and sewing clothes for sale to others — each woman had turned the sum into 12 + 12, 12 + 14, 12 ... always plus. They had gathered that day to repay the loans at 5 percent interest, pleased that the profits would enable them to keep earning cash. The original capital and the accumulating interest were then loaned to women in another village; they, too, would turn the small sum into a working capital in but a few months.

Self-confidence was but one of the results of this micro loan effort. Studies have shown that women's income is spent on better nutrition, home improvements and children's education. Sad to say, men's earnings tend to be spent on less essential consumer items, including visits to vendors of local brew.

The Meri women remind us that "making do with a little" is one of the things that women do well. Stretching family budgets to cover the costs of food, fuel and education is as much a cause for pride in the developing as in the industrialized nations.

The summiteers who spoke so eloquently in Toronto about Third World debt and aid to Africa might take a hint from the village women of the Meri region. If the noose around the hopes and well-being of the poor is to be loosened, the "12 + 12 approach," investing in women's ability to make do, is worth considering.

For too long, women have been brushed off as peripheral to the development of poorer nations. It is called the "cake sale" mentality. Women will always make do; one doesn't have to bother with them.

The proof is there for all to see. The United Nations Development Fund for Women (UNIFEM), the tiny agency which provided the loan in Meri, has a total yearly budget of $7 million. The UN Development Program has $1 billion. For assistance to women — half the population — of the poor world, this smacks not of cake sales but of "let them eat cake."

Prime Minister Margaret Thatcher's government is particularly out of step with women's ability to contribute to economic growth. Last year Britain's contribution to UNIFEM was $90,000, a shameful pittance compared with the Canadian contribution of $1.5 million, the highest of any of the Toronto summiteers.

The Reagan administration has never been particularly enlightened about women's role in society. The U.S. contribution to UNIFEM was $219,000 last year and the administration has halved it in its recent request to Congress. But there are members of Congress who realize that women are responsible for family food production — 80 percent in Africa, 60 percent in Asia, 40 percent in Latin America — and that women are thus essential players in the struggle against malnutrition, infant mortality and poverty. The House Select Committee on Hunger has held hearings on legislation which would give UNIFEM $4 million a year to assist women in increasing food production capability.

The criticism leveled so often at UN management overload is hardly appropriate for UNIFEM. With a staff of 10, it has funded hundreds of projects in the poorest regions of the world which provide direct financial and technical support to women involved in cooperative activities, fuel and water supply, health services and small businesses.

"The point," says the fund's director, Margaret Snyder, "is to get the money into the hands of women, to empower them as agents of change."

She admits that it is not always easy to convince donors of the central role women play in development efforts. "What we try to provide is leverage: leverage monies to individual women, and leverage funds to institutions which should support women's productive capacities."

The Toronto seven discussed billions. UNIFEM's millions are being debated in Geneva this week by the governing council of the UN Development Program. If the summiteers could have visited Meri, or the women of Zambrano, a drowsy river town in northern Colombia, they would have instructed their representatives in Geneva to see to it that UNIFEM graduates from the cake-sale class.

In Zambrano, the women's cooperative has been so successful in producing decorative plants for sale in the cities that young people who had been forced to emigrate to city factories are coming home. In the town they now find jobs, improved housing and far more dignity than in the slums of Barranquilla. The 12 + 12 approach made it all possible.

The writer, author of "Third World Women Speak Out," contributed this comment to the International Herald Tribune.

monopolised this activity.

In the opinion of a UN official, 'The bank has proved decisively that, given a little initiative and backing, the village poor can be relied upon to organise themselves and increase production. And with money comes purchasing power and a higher standard of living.' The success of the Grameen Bank has prompted several developing countries to have a closer look at its operations for possible application elsewhere.[12]

In another successful enterprise, 5,000 Bangladeshi women have formed 520 self-help savings groups by putting aside handfuls of rice which are then sold on the market. With matching funds from Save the Children (USA), they have undertaken income-generating projects such as processing rice, raising poultry, and handicrafts. Some of the profits are used to buy extra food and medicine or to pay school fees, the balance reinvested. Their savings have grown to more than $35,000, a substantial sum in rural Bangladesh.[13]

BANKS FOR MICRO-BUSINESSES ☐

The Self-Employed Women's Association of India (SEWA) was established in 1972 when a group of women headloaders, used-garment dealers, junksmiths and vegetable vendors came together in Ahmedabad to form a workers' association. By 1982 the SEWA trade union consisted of over 5,000 poor women workers; it struggles for higher wages and improved working conditions, and to defend members against harassment by police and exploitation by middlemen. It provides further support through a women's bank, skills training programmes, social security systems, production and marketing cooperatives, and other programmes for developing trades.

The SEWA Bank developed following a decision by the Indian government in the early 1970s to take action on behalf of informal sector workers and small businesses that were normally denied credit in traditional banking. All banks were required to lend 1% of their portfolios to the so-called 'weaker sector'; as a result, SEWA received loans from the Bank of India and other banks, to be administered to poor women. As the success of the bank has gradually increased, so have SEWA's other activities.[14]

Another project for support of micro enterprises has been initiated in Costa Rica by the Banco Popular. The project relies on the solidarity group system, each group consisting of five to eight micro-businesses which join together to qualify for a loan. It has extended loans to 447 clients (of whom 40% were extremely poor, with income inadequate to buy a basic basket of food). Over half the loans were for small stores or street vendors, and one-third for micro industries and services. Each received a loan of $247 for one year.

After one year of operation the project was outstandingly successful. Median income was 145% higher and average income 240% higher, with 119 new full-time and 48 part-time jobs created and increased savings for 60% of the clients. Record-keeping improved and dependence on informal sector moneylenders was reduced. Solidarity increased within the groups, and the payback record so far is good, with only 12% late payments.[15]

TEASHOPS AND TRAINING CENTRES

☐ Virginia Johnstone, of Australia's International Women's Development Agency, reported in December 1987 on a visit to a community in Papua New Guinea, where a business had been set up in 1983 by Huli members of the Tari District Women's Association.

The manager of the teashop, Jacinta

FINANCING

FROM: TRIBUNE NEWSLETTER NO. 18, INTERNATIONAL WOMEN'S TRIBUNE CENTRE.

For those involved in small businesses or income-generating projects, different types of assistance may be helpful...ranging from credit to assistance with marketing, management, quality control or pricing.

Locally, nationally, regionally and internationally, different organizations are trying to provide a broad range of specialized types of assistance. Below are examples of some unique approaches to...

Loans to Individuals:

In Asia, the Philippine Commercial and Industrial Bank has 70 money shops located in stalls in markets throughout the country. To qualify for minimum loans of $125, stall-holders in markets must have daily sales of $7.50 and profits of 25%. Loans are repaid daily. The PCIB reports that the program is so successful that 7 financial institutions are competing for the market.

Small Grants for Start-up Funding

In the Caribbean, Latin America, Africa and Asia/Pacific, the Trickle Up Program (TUP) provides $100 to groups of 5 people or more who have ideas for small enterprises for which: 1) they themselves have planned; 2) 1,000 hours of self-employment can be contributed in 3 months; c) not less than 20% of the profits will be reinvested; 4) more self-employment will be generated. Seventy percent of projects started since 1979 are still functioning.

Start-up Funding to Entrepreneurs

In Bangladesh, the Mennonite Central Committee Action Bag Project provides women who work in their jute-bag production firm with counseling on ways to use money in entrepreneurial ventures. If the woman comes up with an approved plan, MCC will give her $200 to start her own business. Of the 153 women who received funds in 1979, 24 bought sewing machines, 16 invested in rickshaws and others opened retail shops. One year later, 56% were still operating and had improved their incomes.

Haiyape¹, told me how the Women's Association took over an abandoned police lock-up... they originally aimed to use the building for training, but the demand for food and drinks in the area meant that the women could learn how to run a small business and at the same time make an income from sales. This... was a women's community effort; each club in turn sent volunteers to work in the Tari Teashop. The profits were then used to buy supplies and to fund small projects managed by the women's clubs. In this way three clubs set up bakeries in their local communities. Fourteen women have been trained and graduated from the Teashop.

Now it has been decided that increased profits should be spent on building a training centre which can be used by local and provincial women. It will offer courses in nutrition, health, appropriate technology, business management, legal issues and agriculture. The centre will also provide a permanent meeting place for the Association, and be a drop-in centre where women can speak to a counsellor about their problems and needs. To maintain self-sufficiency the facilities will also be rented to other organisations and to the provincial government, to obtain income to cover maintenance costs and salaries of the centre's staff. Additional income will come from providing accommodation for travellers.

IWDA, with assistance from the Australian government's Women in Development Fund, are contributing towards the building of this centre. Other donors are the Canadian High Commission in Canberra, the International Human Assistance Programme (PNG), and the members of the Tari District Women's Association themselves.[16]

HELPING THE NEW ENTREPRENEURS

☐ At the United Nations Interregional Seminar in Vienna on 'Women and the Economic Crisis', consultant Carmen McFarlane of Jamaica pointed to the fact that the enlarged role of women in economic activity, brought about in some instances as a result of a desperate attempt to ensure survival, has created a class of persons like the higglers[17] who, having carved out their place in the total economic activity of the country, are in a potentially more advantageous economic position than they were before the crisis occurred.

It would be in the interests of this new breed of entrepreneurs that pressure be brought on governments to provide some form of support to them to enable them to maintain and even expand their businesses. This has already been implemented by some governments which are now in the process of providing training in areas such as business management, including accounting skills, to the newly emerging class of retailers, service workers and manufacturers. The training provided has so far been very rudimentary but sufficient to enable them to organise their businesses more efficiently.[18]

What are needed are systems supportive of women in their action-oriented approach towards mitigating the negative impacts of economic recession on their lives. They need legislation protecting them at work, consumer cooperatives, child-care facilities near the place of work, and mobile, flexible preventive health care which can reach them at their workplace, at their homes, and where their children are being looked after so that they do not have to ask for time off and risk losing their jobs.

Among the conclusions of the UN Interregional Seminar was one to the effect that the economic crisis, 'while having a negative impact on women in many respects, could provide an opportunity for – indeed, force – a rethinking of approaches to development. Both solving the negative consequences for women and improving the well-being of men and women can be achieved if the full potential of women to contribute to the development process can be encouraged by the policies adopted by Governments.'[19]

1 Permanent Representative of Barbados to the United Nations, in a statement to the UN Economic and Social Council, 14 July 1988.
2 Anita Anand, 'Development in the 1990s: Repetition or Innovation?', *Development Forum*, September–October 1988, United Nations, New York.
3 Marjorie Williams, 'Debt, Deficit and the Fate of Women', *Peace and Freedom*, March 1988, Women's International League for Peace and Freedom, 1 Rue de Varembe, 1211 Geneva 20.
4 Zonta, Mexico: 'Training for Women, a Key to Rural Development,' *Zonta International*, May-July 1987.
5 *Women in Development*. Project achievement reports from UNDP, June 1988.
6 World Food Programme article in *Development Forum*, op.cit.
7 Chris Lewis, 'Transformation through self-reliance', *Development Forum*, op.cit.
8 IFAD, 1985.
9 Richard Longhurst, 'Policy Approaches towards Small Farmers.' *Adjustment with a Human Face*, UNICEF 1987.
10 UNIFEM Occasional Paper No. 4: *UNIFEM Experience of a Revolving Loan Fund*, United Nations Development Fund for Women, New York, December 1986.
11 Advocates for African Food Security task force members, *Women: Key to African Food Security*. Obtainable from UN/NGLS, DC2-1103, United Nations, New York.
12 Priya Darshini, 'Bangladesh Women form Backbone of Unique Rural Bank', Depthnews Women's Feature 20 October 1983; and Frances Stewart, 'Supporting Productive Employment among Vulnerable Groups', *Adjustment with a Human Face*, UNICEF, 1987.
13 Jerry Sternin, 'It can start with a handful of rice', *International Herald Tribune*, 23 May 1989.
14 Frances Stewart, op.cit.
15 Frances Stewart, op.cit.
16 Virginia Johnstone, 'Rural Women Plan for Income and Community Development', International Women's Development Agency Report No.7, Australia, December 1987.
17 See Chapter 10.
18 Carmen McFarlane, 'Women and the Impact of the Economic Crisis', working paper prepared for the UN Interregional Seminar on Women and the Economic Crisis, Vienna, 3–7 October 1988. Doc. SWEC/1988/WP.1, 31 May 1988.
19 1989 Update of the Survey on the Role of Women in Development. Chapter 11, 'Women, Debt and Adjustment'. UNCSDHA/DAW/UNOV, Vienna.

Mozambican refugee, Ukwimi reception centre.

6 DEBT & POVERTY IN ZAMBIA

For Zambia, the principal legacy of British colonial rule was an economy geared overwhelmingly towards the export of copper, with severely under-developed manufacturing and agricultural sectors. Zambia also inherited a debt of over K50 million from the colonial Government;[1] it was one Zambia has never since been able to shake off.[*]

IN THE MID-1970S falling copper prices, combined with soaring import bills (especially for oil) and rising interest rates cruelly exposed the weakness of Zambia's economic structures. Copper still accounted for around 90% of Zambia's exports, and its reliance on imports – it produced few of its domestic requirements – and on copper exports made it particularly vulnerable to falling commodity prices and rising import prices. World recession and rising oil prices have been devastating for Zambia. This huge strain has been magnified by 'destabilisation' in Southern Africa as the struggle against apartheid has intensified. South Africa is Zambia's biggest source of supply (accounting for about 25% of all imports), and over 40% of Zambia's trade uses its transport routes.

In 1978 Zambia turned to the IMF for help, which came – but on very strict terms which, in the event, caused additional economic difficulties and social deterioration, for they were mostly short-term, high-interest loans which came with conditions attached, conditions which in many ways exacerbated the crisis. The currency was devalued, import controls instituted, and wages and salaries frozen. The IMF programme envisaged an easing of Zambia's difficulties as copper prices increased, but they continued to decline and Zambia was left with expensive IMF loans on top of all its other debts.

Since 1982 Zambia has sought help in its adjustment policies from the World Bank, whose objectives have been to decontrol and liberalise the economy so that market forces play a greater role in shaping it, dependence on copper exports is reduced and efficiency improved. But by 1984, the debt service bill rose to $610 million – 60% of foreign exchange earnings. Zambia was in a debt trap and had to start borrowing from commercial banks to meet its debt service bills.

To make matters worse, the donor community started cutting back on its aid and loans. Total medium- and long-term loans and grants to Zambia averaged $569 million a year from 1980–82, and just $315 million p.a. in 1984–85. The decline in real terms is, of course, even more pronounced than these figures indicate. Gripped by an acute shortage of foreign exchange, Zambia accepted in 1985 an IMF proposal to introduce a regular foreign exchange auction to determine a market price for the Zambian kwacha, at that time at K2.23=US$1. In spite of attempts to adjust the system with a lower rate for priority sectors, by the end of April 1987 the kwacha had devalued to K21.01=US$1, less than 11% of its pre-auction value.

Inflationary pressures had grown as import prices rose, and social and political tension became evident as wages failed to keep pace with the cost of living. On 1 May 1987 President Kaunda declared that the IMF programme had failed and announced that it was abandoned. Debt payments to both the IMF and World Bank were suspended. Two months later the government introduced its own 'interim economic recovery plan' which imposed a ceiling on all debt service as a proportion of export earnings. Both IMF and the World Bank had, under their statutes, to stop further lending.

THE HUMAN COST OF ZAMBIAN DEBT □ For the great majority of Zambians the country's debt and associated adjustment packages have combined with recession to produce results which have been little short of disastrous. Devaluation in a country which imports much of its needs means, in effect, a drop in real wages. Wage-earning classes have been pushed into destitution and starvation, and for millions the future looks very bleak indeed.

Zambia's worst poverty is polarised in five of its nine provinces (Luapula, Northern, North West, Eastern and Western provinces) which contain 42% of the population. The most vulnerable groups are female-headed households, children in large (especially rural) households, unemployed youths and people working in the informal sector. In 1980 the five poorest provinces had only 1% of total employment in the manufacturing sector.[2] Although there is widespread and growing poverty in urban areas, on average urban incomes are still 3.5 times rural incomes. The urban poor are mostly engaged in the 'informal sector', which is the reservoir of the under- or unemployed.

Some 52% of Lusaka's informal sector have some paid employment. About 42% of the labour force are involved in petty commodity activities, ranging from trading mealie-meal to selling cigarettes singly and vegetable hawking.[3] Real incomes are declining rapidly as more sellers compete for the shrinking demand and as the prices of urban goods which the poor consume increase. Rising poverty among the young is perhaps the most pressing urban social problem, particularly rural school-leavers

seeking jobs in town.

The kwacha devaluation and the removal of subsidies were key factors in the soaring consumer price index. By January 1987 the purchasing power of the kwacha was just one-third of what it had been in 1983.[4] Against this background, the announcement that the breakfast meal subsidy was to be withdrawn shocked the public. After a weekend of fierce rioting in which 15 people were killed, the full maize subsidy was restored.

At the end of 1987 a World Bank mission to Zambia made a special study of how, if a renewed effort was made to remove food subsidies over a five-year period, the poor could be protected through a carefully designed Targeted Food Ration scheme. The mission tried to establish how vulnerable families would be identified and what role NGOs could play in ensuring that the food reached those families. It was clear that, unless an effective food rations scheme was already in place, the removal of basic food subsidies would be politically and socially impossible. Now the government has publicly announced its intention to phase out food subsidies and introduce ration cards, but it remains to be seen whether such a scheme is feasible in Zambia.

There was a sharp drop in Zambia'a nutritional and health status and a sharp rise in child mortality during the 1980s. UNICEF has estimated that the share of child deaths (under-fives) attributable to malnutrition rose from 29% in 1977 to 43% in 1983[5] – 'a reflection of deteriorating economic conditions and drought.' As hunger and disease increase, the health services have been cut sharply, and the proportion of the dwindling health budget that is spent on primary health care in rural areas and on essential drugs has diminished markedly; maintaining staff levels leaves less and less for essential drugs, bicycle spare parts for rural

CRUSHING STONES FOR A LIVING IN ZAMBIA

Along the Kafue Road, one of the four highways leading into Lusaka, over 300 women, some with babies strapped to their backs, toil from dawn to dusk crushing large limestones into different sizes. Pyramids of stone of all shapes and sizes line the road while others are packed in old polythene bags and sold to Zambia's building industry.

The back-breaking job is 'a punishment for living' says 42-year-old Lillian Daka, who has been crushing stones for almost three months now. 'This iron,' she says pointing to the hammer lying beside the heap of stones, 'has roasted my flesh. But I have no alternative. Either I crush stones or I invite hunger at my doorstep.'

Rising commodity prices have driven women like Daka out of Zambia's capital. Since 1984, when the Government abolished price controls, the price of essential goods has shot up. The only commodity that has kept to a low price is maize meal, because of the public outcry when the Government tried to raise the price. Deep cuts in food subsidies ignited violent riots in the country's copperbelt region.

The Zambian economy hit the doldrums when the world prices of the country's main export, copper, fell to rock bottom. Over two million Zambian youths are unemployed, and only about 300,000 men and women are employed in the formal sector in a country with a population of 6.7 million and whose birth rate rises by 3% a year.

Rosemary Mwale, 41, used to sell agricultural produce in one of Lusaka's markets but when she found she could not afford the prices of her goods she decided to look for work that involved little cost. Last year in November she settled along Kafue Road crushing stones, which are free and in abundance around Lusaka. All one needs is a hammer and the will to crush stones into required sizes.

Many women followed Mwale's example. Lydia Muwowo, a mother of three and a divorcee, said she decided to crush stones after her source of living – street vending – was disrupted by the local council. She used to sell vegetables and buns, but she was under constant harassment from Lusaka's urban district council policemen, who had been instructed to stop street vending as part of a 'Keep Lusaka Clean' campaign. 'I could no longer watch these heartless people throw away the food I was selling. It was painful', said Muwowo.

So far the police have ignored the crushers and in fact the police and some parliamentarians have voiced support for the women. 'Stone crushing doesn't only generate self-employment', says civil engineer consultant Simon Zukas, 'it has the potential to contribute meaningfully to the country's development.'

During a recent debate on estimated expenditure for the Ministry of Commerce and Industry, it was suggested by one MP that the women should be assisted. But Mines Minister Pickson Chitambala was non-committal. 'The matter is very involved', he said.

Meanwhile the women have already improved their earnings since they left their previous jobs. In the markets they earned about US$9 daily, but now they can earn as much as 500 kwachas daily (US$62). As the business gains momentum, says Daka, 'we hope to form a cooperative, so we can produce crushed stones on a large-scale.'

Tiza Banda (Women's Feature Service, Lusaka)
as featured in *Women's World*, March 1988
ISIS/WICCE Women's International Resource Centre, Geneva

workers, and other basic equipment.

Meanwhile government spending on education plummeted as the population increased, falling 62% per capita from 1976 to 1981, a decline in services which has had a particularly serious effect on girls. In 1985 the female illiteracy rate in Zambia was 1.6 times that for males, according to the UNICEF/government of Zambia report.

In the agricultural sector government spending has increased in recent years (as advised by the World Bank), but relatively little assistance has gone to the poorest farmers. This is not only disappointing on humanitarian grounds, it also appears to be economically inappropriate; statistics show that small farmers are economically more efficient even though their yields per hectare are less. Cash income per economically active member of the subsistence farming sector fell by 13% from 1976–85, having 'borne the brunt of the recession in all aspects.'[6] There is still considerable migration to the towns and those left behind (often female-headed households) cannot provide the labour needed for farming, non-farm and wage labour activities.

Improving agricultural prices can help small farmers if they have access to credit, sufficient land, and the extension services they need. For women farmers in particular these questions should be addressed before agricultural prices are increased, and for the urban poor a mechanism should already be in place to safeguard their diet *before* higher agricultural prices are passed on to the consumer. Encouraging more production of marketed, as opposed to subsistence, crops can help the rural economy but can also damage women and children unless attention is paid first to food security. Since this relates particularly to the distribution of wealth within the family, it is vitally important to establish ways of involving women in such agricultural policy shifts.

A NEW PATH FORWARD □ At the end of 1985 Zambia's $4 billion debt comprised of 49.8% bilateral loans (notably from the governments of the UK, US, and the Federal Republic of Germany), 30.4% multilateral loans (more than half of them from the World Bank and one-seventh from the EEC), 13.2% financial institutions (chiefly IMF) and 6.6% suppliers' credits. If it is clear that previous adjustment policies have proved damaging for ordinary Zambians, fortunately new perspectives are opening up.

One is that a new IMF facility has been established (the Enlarged Structural Adjustment Facility) to allow the IMF to make much longer-term loans at very low interest rates. Another is that the IMF and the World Bank are both publicly recognising that adjustment is a more politically sensitive, slower process in Africa than they had thought in the mid-1980s, and that adjustment should be modified to safeguard the interests of the poor from the outset.

The main strands of World Bank thinking, as expressed in late 1986, were: to concentrate on agriculture, health, education and infrastructure maintenance, rehabilitation, fertiliser production, oil pipelines and railways; to increase the salaries of senior civil servants, stem the 'brain drain' to the private sector and redeploy skilled staff to the 'core' sectors; to reduce other unskilled employment; and to resist donor-financed projects outside the core programme.

It also recommended a 12% budget cut (in real kwacha terms, 1986–88) largely to be achieved by phasing out subsidies and cutting non-core sectors, but with a 30% increase in spending on agriculture, a 25% increase in health spending, a 10% increase in education spending and an 83% increase in road building and maintenance (Zambia's roads, mostly built 20 years ago just after independence, are in a very bad state of repair).

The Zambian government has drawn up its own strategy for recovery, the New Economic Recovery Programme, which involves a limit on debt service of 10% of foreign exchange earnings after the forex needs of the mining sector, the airlines and oil and fertiliser imports have been deducted. The government insists that, for Zambia to recover, multilateral debt must be rescheduled; if this is not possible under the statutes, governments of developed countries should be able to buy up this debt. More funds are needed on soft terms. Zambia should be fully compensated for loss of earnings on goods and raw materials (the copper price is the lowest in 55 years, having fallen from $1.95 per pound to 61 cents). Internal reforms include restricting imports to essential consumer goods and to necessary inputs and machinery not available in Zambia. Regional cooperation is to be stepped up. Interest rates have been brought down to 15–20% and the exchange rate fixed at K8=US$1 to control inflation.

The government has announced its intention to diversify its export base away from copper and metals towards manufactured goods, agriculture and gems. Capital-intensive and import-consuming industries will be discouraged in favour of labour-intensive production using local raw materials. Agricultural technologies using abundant land and labour, rather than scarce capital inputs, are to be promoted. Strategies promoting equity include a proposal for a minimum wage, improved primary health-care, and a plan to direct major investments to economically-depressed areas.

The recovery programme has been criticised by aid agency representatives in Lusaka; they say that the government was unwise to stop payments to the World Bank, which had made efforts to ensure that its funding far exceeded Zambia's repayments to the IMF. The break with the World Bank lost Zambia an estimated US$200 million from mid-1987 to mid-1988. Government officials agree that this will have serious repercussions on agricultural development, though at the time of writing a group of Nordic and other donors are considering meeting Zambia's World Bank arrears of approximately US$30 million in order that the Bank can restart lending to Zambia.

OXFAM's recommendations for an appropriate and immediate response to the urgent crisis faced today by Zambia include the following:

1. The British Government should restore the £30 million of aid that it had committed to Zambia in 1987, which it withdrew because of Zambia's break with the IMF, and should seek increased EEC aid funding, especially for poverty-relieving programmes.

2. The international community should give more recognition to the political difficulties faced by the government of Zambia in attempting to stabilise the country's economy.

3. A special debt relief package should be agreed for Zambia.

4. Any future IMF or World Bank lending should be at lower interest rates, with more flexible repayment terms, and carry conditions designed to enhance, not diminish, the well-being of the poor. The impact of economic policy changes on the poor should, in future, be carefully monitored.

5. A determined international effort should be made to help restore Zambia's terms of trade. This would include substantial effort to increase the price Zambia is paid for copper (through international commodity support schemes), opening international markets to other Zambian exports, particularly of manufactured and processed goods, and support for regional trade

initiatives in the Southern and Eastern African regions.

6. Western governments should take as a starting point a careful analysis of the economic effects of destabilisation, in the likelihood that these will be stepped up in the future, and should include a commitment to make a generous allowance for this issue.

If ordinary Zambians like Florence Tambo[7] and her family are not to be made to suffer more than they have already, Zambia needs more aid and more 'debt forgiveness'. The aid should address the pressing needs of the poor, and debt forgiveness should not carry conditions that further reduce their living standards.

JOHN CLARK, WITH DAVID KEEN

OXFAM/UK, MAY 1988*

1 *Situational Analysis of Children and Women in Zambia,* UNICEF/Government of Zambia, June 1986.
2 World Bank reports on Zambia, 1986
3 Guy Mohne, *Employment and Incomes in Zambia in the Context of Structural Adjustment,* ILO/SATEP, Lusaka, 1987.
4 *Consumer Price Statistics,* Central Statistical Office, Lusaka, May 1987.
5 *Situational Analysis of Children and Women in Zambia,* op.cit.
6 Guy Mohne, op.cit.
7 See Chapter 2.

* This chapter was adapted from a paper by John Clark and David Keen.

EFFECTS OF THE CRISIS ON PEASANT WOMEN IN MEXICO

As in other Latin American countries, the economic crisis in Mexico is expressed as a crisis in the growth of productivity, where the rise in the Gross National Product (GNP) has been brought to a sharp standstill. The year 1975 marks the start of the economic crisis which became evident in 1976. At that time two sectors were identified as priorities for action: the farming and fishing sector, to ensure satisfaction of basic food requirements and reduce the deficit in the country's external balance of payments; and energy. As a result there was growing dependence on the export of oil, which in 1981 represented 70% of the country's exports; non-oil exports diminished and foreign debt rose from $29 billion in 1977 to $74.9 billion towards the end of 1985.

DURING THE OIL BOOM (1980-81) speculation and inflationary pressures increased, and growth was due solely to foreign loans, thus preparing the way for future financial catastrophe. Total capital flight had reached about eleven billion dollars shortly before the currency was devalued in February 1982. The situation was exacerbated by the recession which hit the whole of Latin America at the beginning of the 1980s as the economic crisis in the industrialised countries deepened, and by the uncontrolled growth of interest rates and the fall in international demand for oil, leading to further devaluations, a contraction of the economy, galloping inflation and a resulting deterioration in real wages.

The UN Economic Commission for Latin America, in its *Report on Mexico 1984*, estimated open unemployment in the middle of that year at about 13-14% of the economically active population, giving a total of 3.5-4 million unemployed. The proportion of public spending assigned to Social Development fell from 21.1% of the total in 1975 to 13.2% in 1984, while that on agriculture, animal-rearing and fishing was reduced from 11.3% to 5.5% over the same period.

One figure which stands out in this period is that of public spending on administration and defence, which increased from 17.6% to 52.6% of the total. The value of the peso in relation to the dollar went from 30 pesos in January 1982 to around 500 in December 1985; according to national newspapers the government recognised that the rate of inflation for 1986 would be over 100%. During the recent 'Bellagio 3' meeting in Talloires, France, it was stated that, due to the oil price crisis, Mexico has made adjustment involving a reduction of 30% in allocation for administrative expenses and a total stoppage of hospital construction.

THE CRISIS OF MEXICAN AGRICULTURE □

From the beginning of the 1980s, the recession and the financial crisis of the Mexican economy began to have direct repercussions on agriculture. Between 1981 and 1986 the budget for agriculture declined in real terms by 50%. Official investment policies have fundamentally benefited crops relying on irrigation and the more 'profitable' export crops; as a result the production of basic grains for subsistence has been forced to move into zones where the weather is poor and productivity low, land dedicated to these crops has been reduced, and the rate of growth of agricultural production has fallen.

Increases in government guarantee prices were wiped out by similar increases in the cost of agricultural inputs, while the prices of staple food products did not increase proportionately with the prices of fodder and less essential grains. Inflation meant, moreover, that consumer prices rose still further, with a consequent decline in the purchasing power of the worst-off social groups. Peasants at below subsistence level – who are consumers rather than producers of basic grains – found their real wages diminished by 40%.

Transnational corporations are today involved in the production of 90% of processed foods and 84% of animal feeds; their participation in industrial establishments is 31%, but because of intensive use of capital only a relatively small number of people are employed in these industries. Because private and foreign investment has been reduced (−14.2% in 1982 compared with 1981, and −32.5% the following year), the law has been changed to permit foreign capital 100% ownership of certain non-strategic branches of Mexican industry.

The result has been that small and medium-size national companies are being rapidly eliminated by competition from transnational companies; foreign dependence will increase as imports of technology and materials increase; and foreign capital will exercise greater control and influence on types of production in the primary sector and on patterns of consumption, with repercussions on the diet and nutrition of the majority of people in both urban and rural areas.

THE FEMALE LABOUR FORCE □
Among the most dramatic changes which occurred in the 1970s was that of women's increased involvement in farming which, in relation to male involvement, went from 5.2% in 1970 to 6.5% in the 1980s. In some states this increase has been still more marked; in Campeche, for example, the female labour force leapt from 11% of the total in farming and fishing activities in 1970 to 25.1% in 1980. While part of this can be explained by the fact that women began to enter paid agricultural work, it may also be due to a great extent to the increase in women's unwaged work on family farms, caused by the migration of husbands and children, the substitution of work done by wage labourers when the family unit could no longer afford paid labour, and other factors.

Of the 4.5 million day-labourers working in the rural areas of Mexico in the 1980s, one-third are women. Several million more have migrated to the cities, and to work illegally in the United States. There is no doubting the evidence that the 1970s saw a massive proletarianisation of the Mexican peasantry. Moreover, women have been incorporated into the rural proletariat at a faster rate.

Yet only a very small number of young peasant women have obtained paid employment in agriculture, industry or commercial activities in their own native areas, since virtually no jobs have been created in the small rural communities; they have thus been forced to migrate to find work. Only a small number have migrated to the cities, most of them as employees or street sellers. Toward the end of the 1970s, in addition to the increase in women's participation in paid agricultural labour, a new area of paid work began to emerge: the 'putting-out system', or work carried out in their own homes.

DECLINE IN RURAL WAGES □ In
spite of good years in the early 1980s,

Guatemalan refugees are encouraged to participate in income-generating activities.

when agriculture showed growth rates in excess of those for GNP, due to good weather conditions and the fact that, as a result of the devaluations, internal prices of both export crops and crops for domestic consumption increased by more than the overall rate of inflation, the fact is that, in real terms, there was a reduction in rural wages of some 2% for the period 1982-84, during which period the average agricultural wage fell to little more than one-third of the average minimum wage.

Considering the severity of the reduction in real rural wages, which were already so inadequate, and the creation of a vast army of day-labourers, it is clear that the economic crisis must be termed a social disaster in the Mexican countryside. Women have continued to join the mass of day-labourers at an ever faster rate, estimated in 1985 at 1.5 million, many of them single women, vulnerable to sexual harassment or rape and unwanted pregnancies, and to high levels of malnutrition.

Whereas in the past it was common for the day-labourer to migrate, leaving his family at home, today a single wage is inadequate as a family wage and wives also have to look for paid agricultural work. In order to achieve the same purchasing power as the father's wage in 1975, in 1985 the father, the mother and one child had to find paid employment, leading to another disturbing symptom, the reappearance of child labour.

The fact that, since 1982, the national textile industry has been experiencing a severe recession has also reduced wages for homework performed by women –

It may be concluded that, in general terms, the economic crisis has brought about the following changes in the role of women:

1. Loss of home-based income-generating activities such as handicraft and domestic industries. The new work subcontracted to them has replaced only a tiny part of this income, and the crisis has further reduced the income it provides.

2. For mothers, the increase in the migration of husbands, sons and daughters produced by the crisis has meant that the entire burden of farming falls on them in addition to their domestic tasks – a 'feminisation' of small farming.

3. The incorporation of rural women into paid agricultural work alongside their husbands means that they face the most serious social, educational, health, psychological and, ultimately, political problems. The harm caused to these women by massive rural unemployment and underemployment, the drastic fall in living standards, rising malnutrition, the lack of medical attention, poor housing conditions, unwanted pregnancies, rootlessness and the total lack of perspectives for the future, is irreversible, not simply for them but also for their children.

already extremely low since such work is not governed by contract. Physical exhaustion and progressive malnutrition are producing increases in the indices of morbidity and mortality among day-labourers.

---

1 Adapted from *The Invisible Adjustment: Poor Women and the Economic Crisis*, UNICEF, April 1987.

IMPACT OF THE CRISIS ON WOMEN IN THE PHILIPPINES[1]

8

The Philippines is one of the largest debtor nations in the world. The World Bank Report in 1984 on living conditions in the Philippines pointed to worsening trends in poverty, income inequality, employment and real wages over the past ten years, estimating that there were 3.6 million poor families. Under-employment rose from 14.4% in 1971 to 30.5% in the last quarter of 1983.

IN 1984 THE PHILIPPINES owed $27 billion; in the same year there was a 17% increase in the price of petrol and a 27% increase in the price of rice, tinned fish and tinned milk. Inflation was running at 64%. Filipinos blamed the situation on two reasons: deliberate government policy at that time to indulge in a 'borrowing spree', and the open encouragement of such a policy by the lenders. Export promotion raised rather than lowered the economy's dependence on imports, and the story of Filipina women workers' struggle against repressive working conditions made world headlines.[2]

The Philippine economy suffered a major setback in the early 1980s after posting real GNP growth rates averaging 6% in the 1970s. The oil shock of 1979 and the international economic recession which followed greatly influenced the contraction of the Philippine economy. Lower prices for commodities, protectionism, increased international interest rates and much-reduced capital inflows were all reflected in the deterioration of the terms of trade.

In 1983 a structural adjustment programme and an economic and financial recovery plan were adopted. First, there was a sharp curtailment of imports brought about by difficulties in opening letters of credit and limited foreign exchange allocations for imports. The brunt of the import decline fell on capital goods imports. Second, restrictive monetary policy was followed in 1983 to dampen the inflation rate.

The measures had an immediate and significant impact in stabilising the economic situation. Inflation rate was brought down from a high of 50% to 3.8% in 1987. But in real terms domestic product posted negative growth rates of 6% and 5% in 1984 and 1985, recovering slightly in 1986 with a real growth rate of 1.5%, and 5.1% in 1987. Per capita real income declined from a high of P1,949 in 1982, through fluctuations, to P1,683 in 1987. Stabilisation was achieved, but at the expense of slowing down economic activities to a point of stagnation, further exacerbating poverty, unemployment and under-employment and the living conditions of the poor, especially of the rural poor. Indicators show that the female labour force was the hardest hit, in that more than half of the unemployed came from their ranks. Income per capita declined to the 1975 level.

FEMALE LABOUR □ A closer look at the male/female employment data shows that the female employment growth rate displayed wild fluctuations between 1983 and 1986 compared with male employment, implying that women were victims of lay-offs by employers. A unique feature of Philippine employment is the growing number of Filipinos working overseas, from 314,284 in 1982 to

8 Impact of the
Crisis on Women
in the Philippines

449,271 in 1987.

In 1987 40% of overseas contract workers were women, who dominate the entertainment, office work and service sectors. This upsurge is indicative of the difficulties women face in finding jobs in the domestic economy. The very high incidence of women employed as domestic help abroad, the majority of whom have college education, highlights the tremendous pressures on women to find employment. If married, the repercussions fall on their families.

There are about 26,000 women workers in the Middle East and 20,000 more in Japan, Hong Kong and other Asian nations, the great majority classified as domestic helpers. According to a recent study by the Bureau of Women and Young Workers of the Department of Labour and Employment, they suffer extreme degradation, humiliation, sexual harassment and even rape. In addition, they are often faced with hazardous working conditions, including contract substitution, wage discrimination, ill-treatment by employers and other degrading factors.
BERNABE PAGUIO (*WOMEN'S WORLD*, MARCH 1988).[3]

Thirty-eight per cent of total cropland in the Philippines is devoted to the production of coconut and sugar, the country's major export commodities. While agriculture is male-oriented, it is a major employer of women, who comprise 30% of all persons employed in that field. Urban women generally suffer more from the effects of the economic crisis – inflation, unemployment and the general economic downturn – because inflation in metropolitan areas is higher than in rural areas, and unemployment also tends to be high.

POLICY MEASURES ☐ Policy measures taken to address the employment problem of women have the objectives of reducing the unemployment rate of the female labour force; creating income-generating opportunities for women; and providing equal opportunities to women in all endeavours. Specialised programmes are few; among them are the following:

Balikatan sa Kaunlaran (BSK) is a programme of the National Commission on the Role of Filipina Women, a joint undertaking of men, women and youth from the government and private sector working together towards a fuller integration of women in the total development effort of the country. BSK may undertake any development projects based on identified local needs focusing on women's concerns; marketing outlets for Balikatan products have also been established.

Rural Improvement Clubs implement a nationwide education programme to reach women at the village level. It integrates nutrition, home management, family life, agribusiness and human resources development to enhance women's skills and knowledge and their ability to efficiently manage their physical and social environment. Technical assistance and credits are provided through income-generating projects like pig-rearing, poultry-raising, sewing, handicraft, food processing and setting up small retail stores.

The Comprehensive Employment Development Programme (CEDP) was launched by the government in 1986, and was to a large extent responsible for the drop in the unemployment rate from 11.8% in 1986 to 11.2% in 1987. Small-scale community-based projects such as construction of school buildings, water supply projects, farm to market roads, etc. have been given support and funding. Its major elements have now been institutionalised, e.g. the tapping of the population in the area where projects are to be implemented, opening up of the bidding process to the public, and closer monitoring of the projects with the help of the non-governmental organisations. CEDP also redistributes employment opportunities to the rural areas.

Three measures have been adopted by the *Department of Labour and Employment* to safeguard the rights and protect women overseas workers from employer or recruitment abuses: the model contract, or contract review; the pre-departure orientation seminar, providing information on the host country; and the Labour Attaché Office maintained by Philippine embassies in major labour-importing countries to help workers abroad find solutions to their problems.

At home, the *Bureau of Women and Minors* establishes day-care centres, women's welfare facilities and training centres for women to acquire skill and training, and to teach them to be entrepreneurs. And the *Comprehensive Agrarian Reform Programme (CARP)* redistributes lands to tenant-farmers, provides support services such as transfer of technology, irrigation, credit facilities, marketing assistance, rural infrastructure and training. Farming women will be direct beneficiaries of CARP through the improvement in rural living conditions.

A non-governmental organisation, the Freedom from Debt Coalition, was formed early in 1987. It is composed of research-oriented institutions, popular organisations, progressive faculty members from the University of the Philippines, and some lawyers' groups, for most of whom it meant a shift in orientation: for the lawyers it meant taking on economic issues in addition to human rights issues, for popular organisations a shift from basic concerns such as wages, land or prices to tackling a national issue.

The Coalition planned to turn it into a national campaign, broadening membership to incorporate all levels of society, since debt is an intersectoral issue. It has been pressing the Governor of the Central Bank to release information on the debt: how it was used, who borrowed and who lent the sums in question. Members have also been trying to advise and influence policy-makers, but they have realised that, for the campaign to be really effective, it has to have the backing of the people. And, for the people to be empowered, they need access to information and education. This, essentially, is where the Coalition has been investing its efforts and resources.[4]

1 Based mainly upon a study prepared by Juanita Amatong, Assistant Secretary, Department of Finance, Manila, Philippines, for the United Nations Interregional Seminar on Women and the Economic Crisis, held in Vienna, 3-7 October 1988.
2 See Helen Allison, 'Challenging the Debt Crisis', in Spare Rib, issue 176, March 1987.
3 Bernabe Paguio, 'No Bed of Roses for Filipinas Abroad, *Depthnews*, Women's Feature Service, Manila. Published by ISIS/WICCE in March 1988.
4 Conchita Posadas, IBON Data Bank, at the UN/NGO Workshop on Debt,. Adjustment and the Needs of the Poor, Oxford, 19-22 September 1987.

Women in the landscape

Women as fetchers of water, collectors of firewood, tillers of the land and as mothers are usually the first to feel the effects of environmental degradation in the developing world. They are also in the best position to manage the environment but their role is frequently ignored by policy makers and planners.

In Africa, women are responsible for 75% of all subsistence agriculture and 95% of domestic work.

EDUCATING WOMEN

Although the education of women has been shown to have a powerful influence on effective family planning, girls throughout the developing world still receive less schooling than boys. The figures show the percentage of each age group enrolled in appropriate levels of education.

Rich world

Poor world

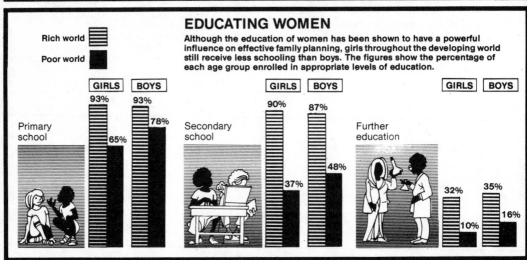

Primary school — GIRLS 93% / 65% — BOYS 93% / 78%

Secondary school — GIRLS 90% / 37% — BOYS 87% / 48%

Further education — GIRLS 32% / 10% — BOYS 35% / 16%

9 PROTECTING THE VULNERABLE DURING ADJUST- MENT: GHANA[1]

During the latter half of the 1960s and 1970s, the Ghanaian economy was caught in the grip of a downward spiral caused by economic mismanagement and adverse external developments. GNP per capita declined in every year except one between 1974 and 1982, during which period constant price GNP per capita fell by 28% amid major food shortages and greatly increased living costs.

THE MOST SERIOUS PROBLEMS were the declines in production in all sectors of the economy and most particularly exports and food. Food self-sufficiency rates – in relation to basic consumption require-ments – declined from 83% to 60% in 1982. With neither commercial imports nor food aid available in adequate volume, by 1982 total food availability was equal to only 68% of estimated minimum basic calorie requirements.

Mineral production declined by 46% between 1975 and 1982, and all manufac-turing output declined by 50% between 1975 and 1981. Output of cocoa, the major source of foreign exchange and a substantial source of government revenue, fell precipitously from nearly 400,000 tons in 1975 to 179,000 tons in 1982. Dwindling government resources led to a dramatic fall in government expenditure; large budgetary deficits and persistent expansion in money supply, combined with declining production and import capacity, generated high rates of inflation.

By 1981 export volume was less than half that of 1975, in large part a conse-quence of domestic policies but greatly magnified by severe adverse developments in Ghana's external circumstances. World prices of major exports fell; combined with the rise in oil price in 1973-74 and 1978-79, this led to a sharp worsening in Ghana's terms of trade. In 1982 the index was less than half that of 1974. In that year Ghana received only $12.6 aid per capita from the international community, compared with $26.1 received by low income countries as a whole in Sub-Saharan Africa. Import volume in 1982 was 36% of the 1974 level.

In 1982-83, the economy was subjected to three further shocks. First, the pro-longed drought and accompanying bush-fires aggravated the already low produc-tion of food crops and created the worst food shortages since independence. Secondly, the sudden influx of about one million Ghanaians from Nigeria in January 1983 put a severe strain on the already critical food and unemployment situation. Thirdly, there was a sharp fall in the price of cocoa. The drought was the worst in living memory; there was a dramatic esca-lation in food prices, which continued to rise until the middle of 1984.

IMPACT OF THE RECESSION ON GHANAIAN HOUSEHOLDS □ Real incomes per head fell substantially. In urban areas high rates of inflation in rela-tion to money incomes drastically reduced real incomes, and formal sector wage and salaried employees were severely affected. By 1980 real minimum wage had fallen to 15% of its 1974 value and continued to fall until 1983. Modest increases in mini-mum wage in 1985 and 1986 notwith-standing, it remained substantially below the 1974 level.

At the worst point following the drought, when food prices were at their peak (June 1984), an estimate of the market cost of a minimum nutrition diet in the urban areas was 168 cedis per person daily. At that time the minimum wage was 35 cedis a day. With the end of the drought food prices declined by about 30% and minimum wages doubled, but this still left a very large gap between household budget requirements for an acceptable diet and the minimum wage.

Open unemployment is not high in Ghana as most people have to find some employment to survive. No household can survive on one minimum wage, and virtually none maintains even moderately acceptable living standards in any public or most private sector families. The stagnation of wage employment which swelled the supply of entrants into the increasingly overcrowded informal sector depressed earnings; most low-income households with a member in formal employment also participate in informal sector activities and in secondary occupations.

Incomes of rural dwellers dwindled because of the fall in agricultural cash crop production and the high rate of inflation. Cocoa farmers' incomes fell substantially after 1970; the 1982 producer price of cocoa was about one-third of the 1970 price in real terms. As a result cocoa was not replanted, disease control was minimal, and even relatively healthy, productive farms were not well tended. Cocoa production, which fell from 413,000 tons in 1972 to 159,000 in 1983, was a major cause of the falls in export earnings and government revenues. While cocoa farmers did shift in part to food production – to some degree limiting falls in their own incomes – this did not lead to a rapid growth of food output, which has risen less rapidly than population over the past quarter.

The World Bank estimated an absolute poverty line in Ghana in 1978 of $307 per capita in urban and $130 per capita in rural areas, when GDP per capita was $390. Roughly 30-35% of urban and 60-65% of rural households were then in absolute poverty. Despite data deficiencies, it is clear that the proportion of households falling below the absolute poverty line is now over 50%.

GOVERNMENT EXPENDITURES IN THE SOCIAL SECTORS ☐ The fall in government revenue, spiralling inflation and the foreign exchange constraint made it impossible to allocate adequate resources to the basic social services – health, education and water. In the health sector, for instance, old equipment in health institutions could be neither repaired, due to lack of spare parts, nor replaced. Basic drugs such as nivaquine and aspirin, and consumables such as bandages, needles and syringes were in desperately short supply. The exodus of health workers worsened an already inequitable distribution of health.

These constraints led to a contraction of health services in a situation where effective coverage was already poor and health status low; in 1977-78 it was estimated that only 30% of the population had access to formal health care, including public and private facilities. Those services available functioned below capacity, incapable of tackling major health problems such as communicable diseases, environmental problems, and maternal and child health including nutrition. Hospital records show that annual attendances dropped considerably.

In rural areas most communities do not have access to good drinking water because many of the boreholes or wells have fallen out of use due to inadequate pump maintenance; they therefore depend on polluted sources of water supply, resulting in a high incidence of waterborne diseases. Parasitic and infectious diseases such as malaria, intestinal parasites, malnutrition and scabies which relate to poverty and under-development have continued to afflict the majority of Ghanaians. In addition, as nutrition and health services declined, diseases virtually eradicated by campaigns in the 1950s and 1960s – notably yaws and yellow fever – began to reappear in the late 1970s with major epidemics.

In the education sector, adversely affect-

ed by foreign exchange shortages and the exodus of trained people, expenditures per capita fell by over 70% from 1975 to 1982. The proportion of trained teachers in elementary schools dropped from 71% in 1976-77 to 54% in 1980-81 because of better-paying occupations both in Ghana and abroad. The education sector lost 4,000 trained teachers within that period. Textbooks, paper and other school materials, teaching aids and school equipment

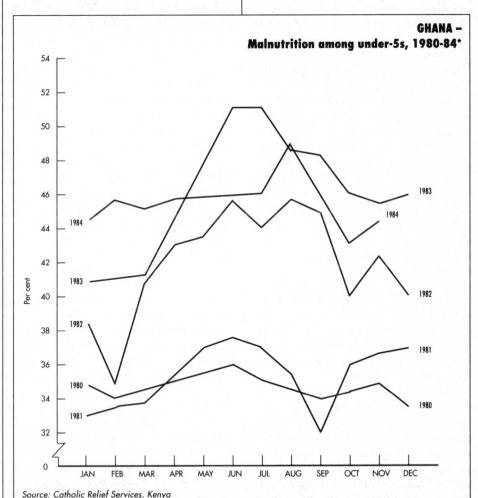

**GHANA –
Malnutrition among under-5s, 1980-84***

Source: Catholic Relief Services, Kenya

*The Catholic Relief Services (CRS) data are based on children attending health posts. Nutritional levels are assessed relative to the Harvard standards of weight for age. The cutoff point used by CRS is whether or not children are below the third percentile of the Harvard standard. The measure is almost identical to the more commonly used cutoff (80% of the median value for weight for age in the Harvard population).

have been in short supply.

The serious deterioration in the quality of primary education is most vividly illustrated by the increase in child labour and drop-out rates. Child labour – in the sense of domestic household chores and agricultural work, especially at seasonal peaks – is traditional in Ghana and need not be inconsistent with child welfare or primary schooling. But as households became poorer, child labour became more crucial to making ends meet. It contributed to the high drop-out rates – especially among girls – as well as to irregular attendance and children too tired to benefit from classes. In the informal urban sector it has been most apparent in hawking and a modern – and much worse – form of 'child pawning' into domestic service to reduce the living costs of poor households.

Government estimates show that per capita food availability in 1982 was 30% lower than ten years before; during the recession, most families were reduced to one meal a day with a very high dependence on cheap root crops, with consequent devastating effect upon the nutritional status of Ghanaians, particularly pregnant and lactating mothers and pre-school children. Ghana's nutritional problem is not simply one of food availability; the main problem for many urban households has been the low level of their real incomes; for rural families too, an increase in incomes is essential for an improved household diet.

Groups most acutely affected by the economic crisis have been low-income households in the urban centres and small rural farmers. In rural areas the most severely affected groups have been small farmers in Northern Ghana, many of them women. Within the households of these severely affected categories, women and children have been especially vulnerable; they have been particularly affected by inadequate food supply, especially during the drought, and other health indicators also demonstrate their low health status. Maternal mortality and infant and child mortality rates are very high; it is estimated that, although children under five account for less than 20% of the population, they account for 50% of all reported deaths; 45% of all infant deaths occur in the neo-natal period due to high fertility rates and low maternal nutrition.

THE ECONOMIC AND HUMAN RECOVERY PROGRAMMES

☐ In 1983 the government adopted a comprehensive package of economic reforms, recognising that 'improving the living standards of the rural populace and the working classes generally is, in the final analysis, the very essence of the Economic Recovery Programme and the ultimate standard by which its success will need to be judged'.[2] Stabilisation policies were backed by IMF stand-by arrangements together with concessional finance from multilateral and bilateral sources. The overall strategy was one of fiscal and monetary measures to promote productivity, production and investment.

The major emphasis of the first stage of the recovery programme was on the productive sectors of the economy, both in terms of the monetary and fiscal measures being implemented and of resource allocations under the investment programme. But in early 1985 UNICEF and the government of Ghana began to study how the welfare of vulnerable groups had changed during the severe economic decline, both before and during the process of adjustment, and what priority actions could be taken to protect basic needs during this difficult period. By the end of 1987, Ghana's 'Programme of Action to Mitigate the Social Consequences of Adjustment', known as PAMSCAD, had emerged.

Attention was drawn to the study during

the first phases of the World Bank's Structural Adjustment Lending missions, and at a special meeting on the human dimensions of adjustment convened and chaired by the government in July 1986, attended by both UNICEF and the World Bank – a meeting which proved to be the decisive point of change. ILO and the World Food Programme joined the two agencies in an inter-agency mission in July 1987, which led to a Consultative Group meeting of donor agencies in Paris in May 1987, followed by an inter-agency mission to prepare PAMSCAD, led by the World Bank and including the WFP, ILO, WHO, UNDP, IFAD, UNICEF and ODA/UK.

The final programme proposal was for $84 million, mostly to be spent over the two-year period 1988-89, amounting to some 6-8% of the estimated annual cost of international support for Ghana's economic adjustment programme. Foreign exchange accounts for about $38 million, about 40% of the total PAMSCAD programme, with some $11 million in the form of food aid. Each of the five main criteria for including projects within the PAMSCAD programme had to show:

- **a strong poverty focus;**
- **high economic and social rates of return or, when this could not be quantified, evidence of cost-effectiveness and support for deepening the social dimensions of adjustment;**
- **modest institutional requirements to ensure speedy implementation;**
- **avoidance of any distortions to the wider goals of the Economic Recovery Programme;**
- **high visibility to enhance confidence in adjustment.**

While PAMSCAD provides a model which can greatly help to protect the poor

and vulnerable in the course of adjustment, it is not without its weaknesses, according to Richard Jolly, Deputy Executive Director of UNICEF. First, it has followed the introduction of the stabilisation and structural adjustment programme by several years instead of being an integral element of that larger programme from the beginning; and the criterion 'avoidance of any distortions to the wider goals of the Economic Recovery Programme' may be difficult to maintain if the shifts of income, production and social services required under PAMSCAD are to take place.

Second, by limiting itself to the short run, PAMSCAD may neglect the wider needs of poverty-focused development over the longer run. And finally, it is not clear how far the model will prove effective in supporting the community-focused, low-cost, local-resource-using participatory approaches that are needed for poverty eradication.

However, in the past few years significant mobilisation of popular support for economic reform has been achieved and belief that economic problems could be overcome has been recreated in the community. Real gross domestic product rose by 0.7% in 1983, over 10% in 1984 and an estimated 6% in 1985. Gross fixed capital information, which had fallen from 12% of GNP in 1982, rose to 6% in 1984 and 8-9% in 1985.

There was also a recovery in development expenditure from 0.5% of GDP in 1983 to an estimated 2.1% in 1985. There have been improvements in cocoa production, and a reduction of external payment arrears despite a sharp rise in debt servicing obligations (including to the IMF) which consumed between 50 and 60% of export earnings from 1985 to 1987, compared with about 12% in 1982.

Revitalisation of community action is an essential mechanism for rehabilitating the social services and developing new initiatives to protect vulnerable groups. Properly tapped, there is a huge reservoir of enthusiasm and potential supplies of labour, materials, even food, which villagers themselves can supply to meet their own needs. Community action has to form an essential part of the strategy to protect vulnerable groups, and may assist in identifying needs, organising a response and part-financing priority projects.

UNICEF, WFP and the World Bank have begun to support programmes for a considerable expansion and improvement in nutrition and primary health care activities. The long-run objective must be that real incomes, land yields and food availability rise sufficiently among vulnerable groups so that households grow enough food or earn enough to meet their food needs without special assistance. Support for local communities to restore and re-equip school buildings, for a project to increase Ghana's capacity to produce basic reading materials, and action in the area of early child development, can be seen as high priorities. The increased necessity for most women to seek work outside the home has made early child-care programmes even more urgent.

The absence of data has proved to be a serious obstacle to identifying problems among vulnerable groups early enough. Monitoring the implementation of the Human Recovery Programme will require improved data collection, particularly on child nutrition, incomes, food prices, food production, and the leading indicators of social stress.

1   Based upon: *Adjustment with a Human Face*, UNICEF, 1987, and Richard Jolly, *Poverty and Adjustment in the 1990's*, Overseas Development Council, 1988.

2   Kwesi Botchwey, Provisional National Defence Council, Secretary for Finance and Economic Planning, *Overview to Progress of the Economic Recovery Programme 1984-86 and Policy Framework 1986-88*, Accra, Ghana, 1985.

10 THE DEBT CRISIS & THE WOMEN OF JAMAICA[1]

Jamaica is the largest of the English-speaking Caribbean islands, approx. 11,650 square kilometres with a maximum width of just over 80 kilometres. It was under British rule, and essentially a plantation society, until independence in 1962. Today, Jamaica has an external debt of more than $3 billion, which consumes 42% of its export earnings in capital repayments and interest charges. This has led its government to seek balance-of-payments support from the IMF, including devaluation, removal of price controls and subsidies, wage restraints and deregulation of the economy, measures which have inevitably fallen more heavily upon the poor.

FOR MOST OF THE PAST TWO DECADES, the bauxite industry dominated the Jamaican economy as the principal foreign exchange and revenue earner – by 1980 it was responsible for one-half of the total foreign exchange earnings. Due to the world economic recession, its contribution fell by more than one-half, to 20%. Heavy reliance on this single industry had left the Jamaican economy dangerously exposed. Tourism and agriculture were not performing at their potential levels, and manufacturing was a net user, not earner, of foreign exchange.

S TRUCTURAL ADJUSTMENT POLICIES

☐ Since 1981 the government has given priority to stabilisation and structural adjustment policies, with the assistance of the IMF, which included aboli-tion of liberalisation of foreign exchange in import controls, domestic anti-inflation programmes, wage control, dismantling price controls and devaluation of the exchange rate.

The trade deficit jumped from $213 million in 1981 to approximately $600 million in 1982-83: while export levels either stagnated or fell over the 1981–84 period, the liberalised import regulations allowed the entry of imports at an unprecedented rate, and were a major contributing factor to the growth of the black market, which in turn placed additional pressure on the exchange rate. This led finally to formal devaluation and the auction system.

In November 1983 the Jamaican dollar was devalued from a rate of US$1 = J$1.78 to US$1 = J$3.15, reaching an all-time low of US$1 = J$6.40 in October 1985. Subsequently the government intervened and revalued to the present rate of US$1 = J$5.50. As would be expected in any economy as dependent on imports as Jamaica, the rapid rate of devaluation had an immediate effect on the cost of living.

S OCIO-ECONOMIC IMPACT

☐ Economically disadvantaged members of society, particularly poor urban women, have been affected especially by price movements in basic foods, most of which had subsidies removed and then prices deregulated. Electricity rates were increased by 116% within a three-month period in 1984, and there have been large increases in the rate charged for other utilities, partially due to the fact that most of the capital expansion programmes were financed by external borrowing.

As a percentage of total expenditure, debt servicing has moved from 26% in 1982-83 to 42% in 1985-86. Retrenchment of staff both in local and central government has had very serious consequences for the provision of social services; hospitals and schools in particular have come under severe budgetary pressures, resulting in partial or total closure or drastically-reduced operating budgets.

EFFECTS OF STRUCTURAL ADJUSTMENT ON WOMEN □ In Jamaica, in

spite of some positive changes, women remain 'the poorest of the poor'. The current population is approximately 2.4 million, of whom 51% are women. Forty percent of women in the 15-19 age group have already had one or two children. A conservative estimate is that one-third of heads of household in Jamaica are women, which means they need an alternative source of income and financial support to provide necessities for themselves and their families, either through employment outside the home or self-employment.

Women constitute 46% of the labour force, 75% of them in service occupations – the sector most affected by the economic crisis – with an estimated 58% in professional, technical, administrative, executive and managerial positions. They are now forcefully penetrating non-traditional technical areas, demonstrating their full potential and capacity to perform on equal terms with their male counterparts. Nevertheless, the majority of Jamaican women work in the informal sector. Two-and-a-half times as many women as men are unemployed, the problem being most severe in the age group 19-24 years.

The impact has been particularly severe on women involved in the production of goods and services, particularly in the agricultural and informal sectors. Many of the women made redundant have embarked on small business enterprises (now referred to as Informal Commercial Importers, or ICIs), the production of non-traditional goods for export, or have become involved in training to retool themselves for other markets. Some have found job opportunities in the Free Zone, but there has been public outcry regarding the conditions of the workers.

Women in agriculture suffered severely, as they did not have adequate access to credit. As poor women they have experienced a reduction in services in the areas of health, education and training and child-care facilities, in some instances having to pay for such services out of their already limited finances. Formal banking systems, such as the People's Cooperative Bank, Agricultural Credit Bank, and the Credit Union Cooperatives, now make provision for women in agriculture and small business enterprises to have access to loans.

At the same time, the government's Solidarity Programme facilitates loans without collateral, on the recommendation of sponsors, to women up to age 30. Private, non-governmental organisations, such as Friends of Women's World Banking, also facilitate loans for women, while others seek funding from both local and overseas donor agencies to facilitate training and income-generating projects for women.

ICIs, OR 'HIGGLERS' □ The ingenuity and dynamism of Jamaican women

continue to manifest themselves as they carve out their own unique recipe for survival. Successive dollar devaluations and wage guideline restrictions have cheapened the price of labour right across the economy, and one of the factors that has allowed Jamaican workers to survive on substantially reduced income over the past years has been the 'higgler'.

Higglers, or Informal Commercial Importers, have used their initiative and drive in a creative and practical way to achieve economic power. Many of them travel to countries such as Panama, North America, Cayman and Haiti with local Jamaican products to trade in exchange for consumer goods which they sell in Jamaica upon their return. They now contribute 60% of the island's domestic economy, and must be reckoned a powerful force. Street higglers have been able to provide cheap food, clothing, footwear and other basic goods that can be afforded by the workers. They have brought in large quantities of imported goods and forced down prices by giving stiff competition to the merchants. They are sensitive to what the lower-income consumers want and go in search of it wherever they can get it at affordable prices.

The growth of the informal sector which the higglers dominate has been part of a new set of survival economic adaptations to the economic crisis. Higglers have not only serviced consumers' needs, they have also provided income and employment for people and families which would otherwise become a burden on the society and the state.

HEALTH AND NUTRITION □ Problems in the health-care sector have been an outgrowth of the problems affecting the nation's economy. By 1979 it was evident that the harsh economic realities of the decade had taken a heavy toll in the primary and secondary health care delivery system. Deterioration was most evident in the physical infrastructure, with most of the health centres and hospitals in a state of disrepair. At the same time, weak management, inadequate supplies, idle facilities, insufficient numbers of trained staff, and inadequate promotional opportunities created a decline in the actual quality of health-care administered to the population. Expenditure cuts emphasised by economic adjustment further delayed the long-needed reorganisation of the island's health care system.

Although it is the government's intention to establish a rational and comprehensive National Health Care Programme, at the present time almost 50% of maternal deaths are thought to be preventable.

Overcrowding in hospitals is leading to early discharge of mothers who ideally are expected to return for post-natal care. Many do not. With the reduction in front-line health staff taking place, there is increasing pressure on health workers.

While it is difficult to assess the effects of structural adjustment on women and children in the area of nutrition, women's cultural orientation often leads them to give boys better meals, and bigger portions, than girls. 'A survey measuring weight/height/age of children under 4 years in two poor neighbourhoods of Kingston found that children with poor nutrition status tended to have poor housing, mothers with low levels of education who worked, and, regardless of other factors, were found to be girls.' (Scott, 1988).

Women, managers of family nutrition, must stretch the household dollar in order to buy food and often deny themselves in order to feed other members of the family. Nutrients needed to maintain women in good health, for normal foetal development in pregnancy, and for lactation are frequently inadequate. As nutritional standards deteriorate, so does physical and mental health. Traditional coping mechanisms are strained, and there is often resort to illegal activities.

One of the most sensitive indicators of the prevailing socio-economic conditions within a country is the nutritional status of its population, particularly that of young children. In 1985 the Voluntary Organisation for the Upliftment of Children (VOUCH), which is supported by OXFAM/UK, estimated that some 50,000 children in Jamaica of three years and under – 28% of the total number in that age group – were suffering from various stages of malnutrition caused by the inability of parents to feed their children because of the economic situation.

A food aid programme launched by the government in May 1984 had two components: the school-feeding programme, intended to provide one 'nutribun' and half a pint of milk a day to 600,000 school-children, and the food stamp programme, providing vouchers to the value of J$10 (approx. US1.80) a month to purchase cornmeal, rice and skimmed milk. However, it is considered to have done little to alleviate poverty or halt the increase of malnutrition.

E DUCATION AND ADULT LITERACY □
The education policy of the government continues to focus on improving the quality and efficiency of education at all levels, and especially of primary education, which is free, compulsory, and provides equal opportunity for both boys and girls to enter the school system. But growing poverty due to the world economic crisis is denying an increasing number of children in Jamaica access to the education system. As food prices go up, bus fares increase, and books and clothing become more expensive, more parents are having to keep their children at home because they cannot afford to send them to school.

Rapid growth in the public sector during the 1970s was seen as a major factor contributing to the balance of payments disequilibrium, and an important objective of the Government has been to reduce public expenditure as a way of meeting IMF requirements. So while poverty decreases access to education, the education system is itself starved of funds. In 1985, an estimated 33% of children – the majority of secondary school age – were not enrolled in any school at all. A much higher proportion were chronically irregular attenders:

'It is cheaper to keep my children at home and feed them from the family pot than to send them to school', said a worker on one of Jamaica's state-owned sugar plantations. She has three children, all of school age. At most they attend school on two days a week, which is all her pitifully low income can afford. The school is not a beneficiary of the government's school feeding programme, which only reaches a quarter of its targeted population. An additional problem is that the school is three miles away and she cannot afford the bus fares. 'The little one aged six gets tired, but what can I do? They must get an education. It's their only hope.'[2]

Funds required to build the targeted 50 primary and 50 secondary schools to meet the requirements of a population which increased by 30% in the decade 1975-85 are simply not available. Not surprisingly, academic achievement is low. An estimated 50% of adult Jamaicans were illiterate in 1984; only one-fifth of students taking the Common Entrance examinations passed, while 66% of 'O' level candidates failed in all subjects and 75% of 'A' level candidates failed to reach the standards required to enter university.

In March 1986 enrolment in the government's adult literacy classes (JAMAL) stood at 12,002, a decline of 22% from 15,464 at March 1985. A skills training programme known as HEART (Human Employment and Resource Training, introduced in 1982) had 300 students participating in 14 courses in 1986.

The process of stabilisation has been particularly hard for Jamaica. The fiscal deficit has been reduced from 17.7% in 1980-81 to 3.2% in 1986-87. But the cost in human terms, and the damage done to the fabric of society, have been astronomical. The situation became even more critical after the severe damage caused by Hurricane Gilbert in September 1988. According to UN sources, an estimated 60 to 70% of the population of metropolitan Kingston, and 40 to 50% outside Kingston, had their houses or shelters destroyed or damaged. Damage to crops is estimated to have been enormous, and power, water and telephone services were almost totally disrupted.

OXFAM, in its Jamaica study, suggests that increased production and expanding opportunities for foreign exchange are long-term processes without which genuine economic recovery is an impossible goal:

'To reduce expenditure significantly in the long term Jamaica has to be in a position to cut back on important levels without impairing the welfare of the people. This can only be achieved if the country can produce and market sufficient food to feed its population and thus reduce its reliance on basic food imports. Again, this is a long-term development goal and part of a profound restructuring of the economy... longer periods must be allowed for debt servicing, and repayment of debt set at a fixed proportion – for example, not exceeding 20% – of export earnings.'[3]

1   Based upon, and adapted from, the following: *Case Study of Jamaica: Women and the Economic Crisis*, prepared by Ms. Patricia A. Sinclair, Director of Women's Affairs, Kingston, Jamaica, for the United Nations Inter-regional Seminar on Women and the Economic Crisis, Vienna, 3-7 October 1988; *Debt and Poverty: A Case Study of Jamaica*, prepared by Belinda Coote for the OXFAM Public Affairs Unit, 1985; and "Debt Crisis", *Women's World No. 17*, March 1988, ISIS-WICCE, Women's International Cross-Cultural Exchange.

2   An interview with Belinda Coote, A Case Study of Jamaica, in *Debt and Poverty*, OXFAM Public Affairs Unit, Oxford, May 1985.

3   Ibid.

11 SOLIDARITY FOR JOINT SURVIVAL

The debt burden which resulted in a net transfer of over US$30 billion in 1986 to the industrialised countries from the developing world – where well over 800 million people live in poverty and misery (beyond any rational definition of human decency), in which over 40,000 children die every day from malnutrition and disease, in which two-thirds of the world's people live – is a scandal.

STATEMENT OF POSITION BY THE EPISCOPAL CONFERENCE OF THE UNITED STATES[1]

OTHER CHAPTERS HAVE DEALT WITH the causes and consequences of the world economic crisis as it affects the rural and urban poor and especially women, and the policies and programmes undertaken both nationally and internationally to overcome the effects of overwhelming indebtedness and structural adjustment policies on the development efforts of societies both North and South. In this section, we look at proposals concerning what can be done by local groups and individuals to spread information about the situation, to encourage action at local levels towards increasing feelings of solidarity and responsibility between communities in North and South, and at national and international levels to prevail upon governments and intergovernmental institutions to adopt alternative policies.

THE MEANING OF CO-RESPONSIBILITY ☐ Because the debt burden is a scandal in which women are the chief – but not the only – victims, it is natural that women, both North and South, should participate in action to correct the situation. Essentially, it is a question of human rights, of cooperation and solidarity, and of insisting upon the human dimensions of what has all too often been seen as a predominantly financial problem. The development activities of many NGOs and UN bodies such as UNICEF over the past decade have been negated by adjustment policies which have undone much of the social progress which had been achieved in developing countries.

The Pontifical Mission's 'Iusticia et Pax' insists that:

The responsibility for forming public opinion to international openness and to the duties of extended solidarity falls upon social, economic, educational and religious leaders, and especially upon politicians, who are all too often prone to assign exclusive priority to national interests instead of explaining to their fellow citizens the positive effects of a more equitable international sharing of resources... Adopting measures to relaunch growth, reducing protectionism, lowering interest rates, and assigning a just value to raw materials all seem to be the responsibility of industrialised countries in contributing to a 'development in solidarity of mankind'.[2]

WIDENING THE DEBATE: THE ROLE OF THE MEDIA ☐ In a guest article published in the IMF/World Bank periodical *Finance and Development* (June 1988), Dr Keith Griffin, President of Magdalen College, Oxford, suggested that in forging an alliance between industrial and developing countries, organisations in the industrialised countries have a role to play:

They can help to educate the citizens of their own country, they can present the facts to the general public, and they can show that the interests of the financial community do not always coincide with those of ordinary men and women. The developing

countries do not need more aid, still less do they need more loans. What is needed is more understanding of where there are harmonies of interest (in accelerating growth, in promoting peace, in safeguarding human rights, in protecting the world's ecology).

Where conflict of interest is unavoidable, as over the issue of unilateral action, what is needed is greater clarity as to the responsibilities for the present state of affairs, whose interests will be damaged by a particular course of action, and whose needs on grounds of equity deserve highest priority. If an agreed cooperative settlement of the debt problem cannot be negotiated, unilateral action, including partial default, by debtors may be one course of action. The much preferred course, however, would be one based on the long-term interests of creditors and debtors in the context of a negotiated, cooperative solution of the debt problem.[3]

There is indeed a great deal to be done to inform and educate people, both North and South, about the true facts of the world economic crisis. As an editorial in the *New Yorker* (4 July 1988) put it:

Third World debt is not a subject that most Americans have given much thought to. Indeed, it has intruded upon our collective consciousness in recent years only at moments of crisis. Not until 1982, when major debtors like Brazil and Mexico threatened to default on their obligations – thus raising the spectre of instability within the world financial order, not to mention enormous losses for American-based multinational banks – did news about Third World debt come to be featured on the front, rather than the financial, pages of our newspapers.

Suggesting that the view from air-conditioned offices in Washington and New York is not necessarily the same as that from shanty towns outside São Paulo and Manila, the *New Yorker* noted that developing nations owed creditor governments and institutions in the Northern Hemisphere over a trillion dollars.

While that's not an enormous sum in today's global economy (our own country's public debt is twice as large), for these nations it is a crushing burden: it not only creates much lower living standards, especially for the poor majority, but also makes the economic growth that is necessary for climbing out of debt even harder to come by. Only the most optimistic analysts expect that the debt will ever be repaid in full. Even the cost of servicing it is tremendous. Between 1982 and 1987, poor countries transferred a net total of a hundred and forty billion dollars in interest payments to rich countries – the equivalent of two Marshall Plans. The austerity measures imposed upon debtor nations to enable them to make these payments have had a frightful human cost.

The *New Yorker* article refers to Susan George's recently published *A Fate Worse than Debt*[4], in which she explains that one of the IMF's primary requirements of indebted countries has invariably been that they reorient their economies to maximise exports. The ostensible aim of that strategy is to earn the cash needed to pay off outstanding debt. The actual outcome, however, is often quite different. Because so many poor countries find themselves in the same predicament, they all end up trying to export at the same time. The consequence has been a glutted world market for most raw materials and, in turn, the lowest commodity prices in some fifty years.

'This debt burden punishes the United States as well,' continues the *New Yorker*.

When developing economies are squeezed dry to pay off foreign bankers, less money is left to import products; according to some experts, the drop in this country's exports to Mexico alone since 1982 has cost at least a quarter of

a million Americans their jobs. In a perverse sort of way, this may be hopeful news – if only because it gives the United States fresh incentives to tackle the problem ... but even if much of the debt is cancelled, there is scant prospect for genuine improvement unless debt relief is linked to new and creative development strategies that will help the impoverished majority in the Third World help themselves. Only then is real growth likely.

An article by Alan Riding in the *International Herald Tribune* of 30 November 1988 also raises the alarm:

Although the debt burden has been choking economic growth for half a dozen years, Latin American officials are now warning that in country after country falling living standards are breeding a hopelessness that is beginning to translate into ominous political decay. Many experts in Latin American affairs even believe that unless the region's scarce earnings can be channeled away from foreign debt payments and back into economic growth, military takeovers cannot be discounted in the next year or two in several countries that only recently returned to civilian rule.

Indicating that these debt repayments were running at about $30 billion a year, Mr Riding pointed out that, 'like Latin American nations, the United States is also a major debtor, its debts to foreign creditors totalling nearly four times Brazil's liabilities. Unlike Latin American nations, the United States has a major advantage because its debt is in dollars, its own currency, which reduces the leverage that foreign creditors exert over US policies. Washington is increasingly worried about the seeming intractability of the Latin American debt problem because these

nations represent a significant market for American goods, normally accounting for up to a third of US exports.'

Articles like these, and books like that of Susan George, do a great deal to inform and educate the public about the problem. But still too little is known about the fact that it is women who bear the brunt of the burden of adjustment. Thousands of words have been written on the economics of recession and adjustment, but careful analysis of the impact on women has been largely missing.

According to Dr Richard Jolly, in a statement made at a UNDP Roundtable held in Budapest in September 1987.[5]

Women's studies have tended to focus on the longer-term trends in women's position but have neglected how these trends have been affected by the sharp shift from economic growth, however inadequate, to economic stagnation and decline. So there is a real need for more empirical data on how the situation of women has been changing and for more careful analysis of the links between these changes and recession and adjustment.

NGO SUGGESTIONS FOR RAISING AWARENESS □ A UN/NGO Workshop on 'Debt, Adjustment and the Needs of the Poor', held in Oxford from 19-22 September 1987, brought 58 representatives of Northern and Southern NGOs involved in education and campaigning, research and training and/or operational work, together with six UN agencies (ILO, UNICEF, UNCTAD, UNDP, WFP, World Bank) and the Canadian International Development Agency (CIDA), to discuss the crisis.

A final statement by the NGOs, agreed at the closing plenary, made proposals for action in both industrialised and developing countries. It described the nature and dimensions of the crisis and its impact on the poor, and made proposals for action at the international level (debt and debt management), at the domestic level (adjustment policies taking into account the needs of the poor), for monitoring the

adjustment process, and for development education and action in both North and South.[6] (See also Chapter 4.)

The NGO proposals were made with a view to strengthening the voice of Southern grass-roots organisations in the design and implementation of the strategies which shape their future, and to generating a process of consensus-building, both North and South, which would support and make possible the implementation of the action proposals. These were:

1. Support for Third World government initiatives to launch a process of debt relief, through the imposition of ceilings on their debt service bill and the adoption of measures to ensure that foreign exchange is allocated to priority development efforts designed to reduce poverty.

2. Development, through a consultative process, of a code of conduct or framework of ethical principles to govern debt management. This code should also address Northern governments' responsibility vis-à-vis commercial banks and official financial transactions.

3. A campaign for increased responsibility on the part of commercial banks for the social effects of their loans to Third World countries, establishing relations with socially-concerned shareholders who can campaign for the introduction of such control mechanisms.

4. A campaign to mandate the International Court of Justice, or a specially constituted international tribunal, to adjudge the possibility of repudiating loans for ill-advised development projects, not incurred by the governments currently charged with honouring the debts, and to allocate the financial burden to those banks and industrial corporations identified as being at fault.

5. Exploration of the advantages and disadvantages of 'debt-for-development' swaps, examining the conditions under which Northern governments and NGOs can use such mechanisms to benefit the poor.

6. Use of the occasion of the Annual Meetings of the International Monetary Fund and the World Bank, and the Paris Club meetings on the official debt of developing countries to present their evidence of the impact of the debt crisis on the poor and to lobby for appropriate debt relief.

7. Further pressure on Northern governments for a comprehensive programme of debt relief to ease the burden of official debt service of low-income, IDA-eligible developing countries, and to ensure that tax relief granted to commercial banks who make Third World loan loss provisions contributes to lightening the burden of specific debtor countries.

8. Increased pressure on Northern governments to honour commitments entered into with Third World governments through multilateral negotiations, such as in the Substantial New Programme of Action for the Least Developed Countries, the UN Programme of Action for African Recovery and Development, and the Final Act of UNCTAD VII.

9. Action by Third World NGOs to bring to the attention of their governments the alternative policies identified at the national level, and to convince these governments of the need to pursue inward-looking strategies towards self-reliance and the satisfaction of basic needs; and action by Northern NGOs to campaign for increased support from Northern governments for the implementation of such strategies.

10. Establishment of guidelines for policy dialogue between NGOs, the IMF and the World Bank, in particular to expose these institutions to the perspectives of the poor and of grass-roots organisations in the Third World; and of a common agenda for a simultaneous international lobby on the issues identified in the Final Statement.

3 Overseas corporations: A high proportion of trade in primary products is controlled by multinational corporations, who dictate the price paid for the products. They also control much of the local economy and culture.

2 Development of cash crops: The need to pay for imports and for the repayment of loans brings government encouragement of cash crops, usually on the best farming land.

4 Development: There are broadly two forms of development. One involves ordinary people, meets their own needs and uses technology which they can control. The other form is based on Western technology and imposes foreign solutions.

5 Arms imports: Over the last 20 years developing countries have imported weaponry worth $223 billion, equivalent to three quarters of all arms imports in the world.

6 Debts: Almost all Third World countries are heavily in debt to the Western banks and governments. In 1983 they paid the West $21 billion on debt servicing – seven billion more than they were able to borrow that year.

START HERE

1 Colonialism: One result of nineteenth century colonialism was the forced development of cash crops to meet the ruling country's needs – for primary goods like cotton or minerals for its factories.

7 Loans from the IMF: Countries that cannot service their loans and need extra time generally talk with the International Monetary Fund. The IMF is dominated by the USA and other Western industrialised nations which insist on an austerity budget. The effects on the poor are serious.

16 Drought and other disasters: There have always been natural disasters. The present disasters however, hit people already weakened by cycles of exploitation and the effects are much worse.

8 Urban unrest: The gradual destruction of the economy brings disaffection, and can provoke unrest. Rioting in the city leads to publicity and pressure on the government to do something.

HIGH RISKS

A gripping game of chance involving the governments and peoples of the developing world.

15 Migration to cities: Tractors are displacing farm workers and the rural unemployed are moving into towns. In 1985 31 per cent – more than a billion – people lived in Third World cities. By 2000 AD this will be two billion.

9 Overseas aid: Help takes many forms. The most valuable supports the local economy. Less helpful is aid for sophisticated foreign machinery, and as business investment or aid as a loan.

14 War: There have been around 120 wars since 1945. Almost all have been in the Third World, and most have been civil wars – at least in part. In 95% of these conflicts there has been outside intervention, mainly by the superpowers.

13 Repression and military rule: Faced with increasing unrest, governments resort to repression and military rule. By 1985 out of 114 independent developing states, 57 were controlled by the armed forces.

12 Rural unhappiness: widespread hidden hunger. Farmers are forced to accept low prices for their crops from government to feed the towns.

11 Drop in food production: By 1985 Africa was producing only 91% of the food it grew in 1975, an average year. In contrast, both Asia and Latin America were growing substantially more over the same time span.

10 Cheap food policies: It is easier to riot in the towns than the country, so governments try to keep townspeople contented. One way is through cheap food. Some may be imported, the rest comes from the rural areas.

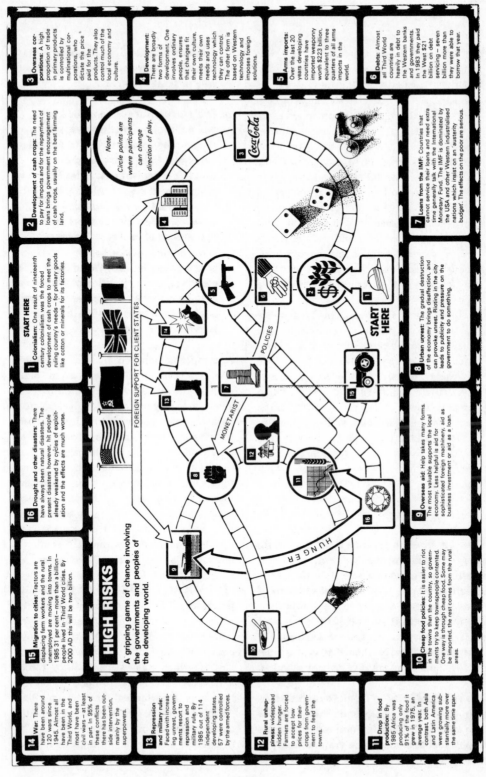

Note: Circle points are where participants can change direction of play.

FOREIGN SUPPORT FOR CLIENT STATES

POLICIES

MONETARIST

HUNGER

START HERE

It was also agreed that NGOs in North and South should strengthen their networking activities to identify changes which need to be effected in Northern societies and economies in order to ensure effective design and implementation of development strategies for the poor. They should also share on a global basis the information, data and analyses collected in their efforts to monitor the impact of adjustment policies and programmes on the poor, working in a more concerted manner to disseminate and use the results of their monitoring to influence adjustment policies and programmes and the institutions and governments responsible for them.

In January 1988 a Debt Conference took place in Lima,[7] organised by the Liaison Committee of European Development NGOs and Peruvian NGOs. The 220 participants also included representatives from Latin-American trade union organisations, people's movements, church organisations, lawyers and economists; Canada and the United States were also represented at the Conference. Non-governmental organisations from both North and South established a common action programme and agreed to work on three main fronts:

1. The legal front: to promote initiatives which challenge the legality of the debt, with particular focus on the International Court of Justice in The Hague. Initiatives include establishment of teams of lawyers in each indebted country to coordinate their activities with those of NGOs and people's movements, and encouraging the establishment of an international 'People's Court' to give a legal judgment on what is morally payable.

2. The social and ethical front: to capitalise on existing strength, namely coordinate NGO activities with trade unions, the churches and other people's organisations, and associate them systematically in their lobbying campaigns, e.g. for a Decade of Grace

during which the debt would be cancelled – a project already under way in some countries.

3. The economic front: to lobby banks and multilateral institutions, and to support the creation of an 'Indebted Countries' Union' composed of people's organisations, to lobby international organisations with regard to a New International Economic Order. Also support for a reappraisal of producers' unions, trade union participation in preparations for IMF/World Bank meetings, and acquisition of hard-core data on activities of governments and banks with a view to a North-South information exchange.

A campaign launched by War on Want (UK) in 1986 had in fact asked bank users in Britain, development groups, local authorities, religious organisations, political parties, unions and women's organisations to press the banks and the government to ensure that solutions to the crisis favour the poor, that banks reduce their demand for payments on existing debts, that new finance be made available on terms which ensure that the poor benefit most, and that new measures be taken to expand the world economy to the mutual benefit of developing and industrialised countries.[8]

ADVOCATES FOR AFRICAN FOOD SECURITY ☐ To promote action to ease women's burdens, representatives of non-governmental organisations and governmental and UN development agencies have formed a special task force: Advocates for African Food Security: Lessening the Burden for Women. The Advocates held a special Symposium during the meeting in New York of the UN Mid-Term Review of the implementation of the Programme of Action for African

Economic Recovery and Development. It was opened by Ruth Engo (UNIFEM) of Cameroon who made a strong plea for investment in African women farmers:

Women farmers are central in the struggle to end hunger, central in the protection of their families' health, central in encouraging the learning process, central in building confidence and self-esteem for the next generation of Africans and, overall, central in improving African human resources physically and morally. This means that they are the central focus for growth. Therefore investing in women farmers of Africa is investing in hope.

The 175 participants at the Symposium put forward a number of proposals for continuing or enhanced action by NGOs, bilateral and multilateral donors, and governments, including that they should:

- **Measure and assess the degree of involvement of women in national, regional and international bodies to obtain data for use in planning and advocacy.**
- **Ensure that women are equitably represented in all African NGO programming in direct proportion to the amount of food produced.**
- **Urge elected representatives and parliamentarians to support aid programmes that lessen the burdens of women.**
- **Contact officials in charge of development programmes and ask how these activities are helping African women farmers become more productive, while at the same time increasing their well-being.**
- **Support UN resolutions and actions that assist African women farmers, and contribute to organisations that are committed to aiding them. Seek out**

grassroots African organisations working with and for women farmers and offer to co-fund projects and programmes.
- **Earmark support for relief programmes that lessen the burdens of women. Ensure that relief food will not compete with local production.**
- **Promote development education programmes to create awareness and understanding of African farm women's needs, roles and potential. Write articles for the local media, organise study groups, and develop networks for cooperative action with African NGOs working for or with the woman farmer.**

Virtually all the donor government submissions and statements to the Mid-Term Review recognised the need to reduce Africa's debt burden, improve Africa's trading position and increase resource flows to Africa. The World Bank representative, focusing on 'Africa's main development asset – its people', said that in recent years the need to protect vulnerable groups affected by the transitory costs of adjustment had been a prime social policy concern:

We must strive to more fully integrate social policy and the growh effort. Improved health and nutrition, education and training, access to family planning services and the full involvement of women in the development process all contribute strongly to economic progress...'

WOMEN'S GROUPS IN ACTION □

Women's groups at both national and international levels are active in assisting community groups to raise awareness about structural adjustment. In the South, as important as self-help projects are the national networks that provide educational or cultural support, such as the Federation of Shantytown Housewives of La Paz, Bolivia, and Sistren in Jamaica, who work through drama to raise awareness among women. Women's groups in Peru have produced booklets in cartoon form on legal rights for semi-illiterate women, and women in Africa and the Philippines are organising to press for changes in the priorities of their governments.

The primary activities of the African Women's Communication and Development Network (FEMNET), which grew out of the African Women's Task Force organised at the 1984 Arusha Regional Preparatory Meeting for the 1985 Nairobi NGO Forum, are identification, documentation and research on women in development issues. The Wamama African Research and Documentation Institute (WARDI) in Kenya focuses on action-oriented research and training to develop women's professional and entrepreneurial capabilities, and to make development more effective in improving women's lives. In Ghana, a Women's Credit Union has been established by the National Council on Women and Development to help women save and invest in projects they choose. Women's World Banking provides hands-on management assistance to newly organised affiliates, and now has programmes with 92 groups, all organised and led locally, enabling women entrepreneurs to obtain capital and learn management skills.[10]

Other international women's networks, such as ISIS/WICCE (Women's International Resource Centre, Geneva) and DAWN (Development Alternatives with Women for a New Era) are undertaking development education and action work with women's groups in both North and South. DAWN, WAND (Women and Development Unit) in the Caribbean, and AAWORD (African Association of Women for Research and Development) in West Africa, combine research and practice in order to evaluate standard macro- and micro-economic analyses, document their negative impact on women, and develop alternative frameworks.[11]

DAWN, for example, has carried out extensive research into the effects of the economic crisis on women in developing countries, in collaboration with women's groups of researchers in those countries. Neuma Aguiar, Coordinator of the DAWN Network, participated in a 'Meeting of Private Agencies and Networks Working to Benefit Women in the Latin American and Caribbean Regions' which took place, under UNICEF sponsorship, in Bogota, Colombia, in December 1986. Subsequently, on behalf of the DAWN Latin American Region Research Group, she prepared a paper relating to *The Impact of the Latin American Crisis on Women*. The paper represents a summary of the analysis carried out by several researchers; the following excerpt gives a description of women's movements in Latin America which are dealing with this theme:

Major communication strategies with poor women are being established by several feminist networks; the Centro de Estudios de la Mujer in Chile and in Argentina; La Morada, also in Chile; Flora Tristan in Peru; CIPAF in the Dominican Republic; IDAC in Rio de Janeiro; the Rede Mulher in São Paolo, CEAAL throughout Latin America; the SOS Corpo in Recife and innumerable other groups have maintained a systematic service addressed to the poor. DAWN has begun to provide basic research information to these groups so as to... provide them with one analysis of problems they currently face.[12]

Researchers from six Asian countries met in July 1988 in Tagaytay, Philippines, to develop a plan for research on the impact of food, energy and debt management on various classes and groups of rural women and men, develop alternative visions of development, and examine new strategies

A CONVENTION...
FROM IDEA TO IMPLEMENTATION

ISSUE IDENTIFIED

INTRODUCED TO UN BODY

DISCUSSION

REPORT DRAFTED

DECLARATION RECOMMENDED

SECRETARIAT PREPARES DRAFT

DECLARATION ADOPTED IN COMMITTEE & FINALLY IN UN GENERAL ASSEMBLY

SOMETIMES GOES DIRECT....

CONVENTION RECOMMENDED

SECRETARIAT PREPARES DRAFT

CONVENTION ADOPTED IN COMMITTEE & FINALLY IN UN GENERAL ASSEMBLY

OPEN FOR SIGNATURES AND RATIFICATIONS OF COUNTRIES

COMES INTO FORCE ON RATIFICATION BY SPECIFIED NUMBER OF COUNTRIES

IMPLEMENTATION

PEOPLE AT LOCAL LEVEL

1 2 3 4 5 6 7 8 9 10 11 12 13

FROM: *RIGHTS OF WOMEN WORKBOOK, INTERNATIONAL WOMEN'S TRIBUNE CENTRE, 1983.*

for shaping development alternatives. The group's work was used at a DAWN inter-regional meeting held at the end of 1989. The research and publicising of such analyses, and close monitoring of the situation of women in crisis situations, are essential if national and international debt and development policies are to change. Women's groups at local and national level are key partners in such monitoring.

CHANGE, a women's group in the UK, carries out development education work in that country in collaboration with women researchers in developing countries, while American members of an international women's network proposing to organise a Women's Alternative Economic Summit have suggested that such a meeting aim to (1) build national voices which articulate a concept, theory and practice of economic development based on women's personal experience; (2) co-ordinate action for change by seeking to unify women as a powerful political force in developing economic policy and decision-making; and (3) establish national networks to promote grassroots economic literacy among women and to build understanding of the links between personal experience and the global economy and between political and economic analysis.[13]

The world economic crisis is everyone's concern, but perhaps especially the concern of women, since women are those who suffer most because of unemployment, food shortages, high prices, and work overload. But poor men suffer too, and so do children, both male and female. Unless a durable solution is found to the question of national indebtedness, adjustment difficulties, and the serious imbalance in world trading mechanisms, the number of people affected by the economic crisis, both North and South, will grow at a disastrous rate.

This book has tried to present as many as possible of the views and analyses relating to the world economic crisis and its impact on women, as well as the broad range of opinions and suggestions concerning possible solutions to the problem. Hopefully it will help groups and individuals concerned about development and women's issues to come to grips with the questions of debt and adjustment policies as they relate to women, both North and South; to consider possible solutions, and how they can contribute to their realisation; and to learn of the ways in which other individuals and groups have added their voices to those trying to draw attention to a crisis which has every chance of becoming a time-bomb unless urgent action is taken to defuse it.

The activities of organisations, women's and youth groups, and schools at local and national levels can do much to encourage a solution to this grave problem, and often results in important initiatives being taken; for instance, public pressure led to the report prepared for President George Bush by a bipartisan commission headed by former Presidents Ford and Carter, listing the debt problem among those requiring 'immediate decisions and actions'.[14] (See Chapter 3.)

Actions at local and national levels constitute the building blocks for effective action at the international level. And while individuals who are not politically, economically or socially active on one of these levels – for example, as a government official, a member of parliament, an official of local government, a trade union leader, a well-known businessman or woman, a religious or educational leader, official of a non-governmental organisation or leader of a women's or development group – may feel that they have little influence in matters of this kind, it is in fact the combined voices of those who care, and who express their concerns, that often tips the balance.

1   CIDSE (International Cooperation for Development and Solidarity, Position Paper on *Third World Debt*, early 1988. (See Part 2: Policy Responses).

2   *At the Service of the Human Community: An Ethical Approach to the International Debt Question.* Pontificial Commission 'Iusticia et Pax', Vatican Polyglot Press.

3   *Finance & Development.* IMF/World Bank Publications, Washington, June 1988.

4   Susan George. *A Fate Worse than Debt,* Penguin, 1988.

5   Richard Jolly, *Women's Needs and Adjustment Policies in Developing Countries*, UNDP Roundtable on 'Managing Human Development', Budapest, 6-9 September 1987.

6   UN/NGO Workshop on *Debt, Adjustment and the Needs of the Poor*, 19-22 September 1987. Final Report, UN Non-Governmental Liaison Service, Geneva.

7   NGO Conference on *External Debt. Development and International Cooperation*, Lima, Peru, 25-29 January, organised by the Liaison Committee of European Development NGOs and Peruvian NGOs. The 220 participants also included representatives from Latin American trade union organisations, people's movements, church organisations, lawyers and economists; Canada and the United States were also represented at the Conference.

8   Helen Allison, 'Challenging the Debt Crisis', *Spare Rib*, March 1987. See also Allison, 'The International Debt Crisis – Women the Hardest Hit, *Women's World* No. 17, March 1988, ISIS/WICCE, Women's International Resource Centre, PO Box 2471, Geneva.

9   *Africa and the United Nations*, An overview prepared by the UN Non-Governmental Liaison Service, Geneva, March 1988.

10 *The Women's Watch*, Vol. 2, No. 1, March 1989. Published by International Women's Rights Action Watch, eds A.S. Fraser and M.A. Freeman, University of Minnesota, USA.

11 Marjorie Williams, 'Debt, Deficit and the Fate of Women', *Peace and Freedom*, March 1988. WILPF, 1 rue de Varembé, 1211 Geneva 20.

12 Neuma Aguiar, *Impact of the Latin American Crisis on Women*, Development Alternatives with Women for a New Era (DAWN), rua Paulino Fernandes 32, Rio de Janeiro, Cep. 22.270, Botafogo, Brazil.

13 'The Global Economic Crisis, Structural Adjustment and the Fate of Women,' draft of a concept paper for a 'Women's Alternative Economic Summit.' *Debt Crisis Newsletter*, Vol.3, No. 1, March 1988.

14 *International Herald Tribune*, 6 December 1988.

ANNEX I

DEFINITIONS OF KEY TERMS

adjustment the process of responding to (often severe) imbalances in the economy, particularly deficits in a country's balance of payment, usually by adopting measures which expand exports, reduce imports, or otherwise attract foreign exchange to a country. Often, measures to curb a government deficit by increasing government revenue or reducing expenditure are also involved. These actions involve changes in the structure of the economy.

adjustment policy a purposeful and coherent set of policies towards the goal of economic adjustment. Since the goal of reducing a deficit can be achieved in different ways, and over different time periods, one can speak of a short-term adjustment policy, growth-oriented adjustment policy, or an adjustment policy focused on growth and human needs (thus, 'adjustment with a human face').

auction system the auctioning of convertible foreign currencies by the central bank, which involves a fluctuating exchange rate for the national currency and determines priority sectors to which such foreign reserves can be applied.

balance of payments a set of accounts for a given period, usually a year, which summarises the financial transactions of the institutions and residents of one country with the institutions and residents of the rest of the world. The set of accounts consists of a current account which shows expenditure on the purchase of goods and services from abroad, and the revenue derived from the sale of goods and services to the rest of the world; and a capital account, which shows the flows of private and public investment and of other transfers and measures changes in domestic and foreign capital assets and liabilities. Bilateral loans and government contributions to multilateral lending agencies are part of the capital account; bilateral grants, all technical cooperation and other multilateral flows are part of the current account.

capital flight funds that leave a country, either in the form of foreign investment by private individuals and corporations, or deposits in foreign bank accounts.

commercial (private) debt debt owed to private creditors, such as commercial banks or suppliers.

compensatory financing facility an IMF facility which provides compensatory cover to overcome a temporary shortfall in export receipts which has arisen due to circumstances largely beyond a country's control. It can also be used to cover temporary excesses in cereal imports due to drought, hurricane damage, etc.

concessionality the degree to which the terms of a loan result in a smaller return to the lender than the normal return

from the commercial investment of the funds.

conditionality the obligations accepted in relation to developing countries' policies or institutions as part of an aid transaction.

conversions to grants and moratoria on repayments an option which has particular relevance to aid-related debts. Former British Chancellor of the Exchequer Nigel Lawson has proposed that sub-Saharan African countries which are following approved economic reform programmes should be eligible for the conversion into grants of all government aid loans, longer rescheduling periods and longer grace periods, and the reduction of interest rates by between 2% and 3% below market rates. This proposal would not affect the debt owed to the multilateral financial institutions, which are not permitted by their statutes to write off debts.

debt capping the favoured solution of several Latin American and some African countries, involves placing a ceiling on the level of export earnings that will be used to service debt. It can lead to problems regarding access to credit for imports, as in the case of Peru.

debt-conservation swaps pioneered by US-based Conservation International, and operated in a similar way to debt-equity swaps. One involved the purchase of a large tract of the Bolivian Amazon forest, using part of the Bolivian debt, bought on a secondary debt market and resold to the Bolivians for its face value in local currency. (See secondary debt market.)

debt-development swaps offered to both bilateral and non-governmental organisations by private banks; debt is purchased on the secondary market and resold to the debtor government for the full face value in local currency, which in turn is invested in development projects. Both ethical and practical questions arise, not least the need to have government approval for the scheme to go ahead, which may limit the available development projects and partner options.

debt-equity swaps involve the debtor country exchanging loans for equity investments inside the country with the effect of reducing servicing costs. They are small-scale (approaching $6 billion) and generally recognised as providing at best a partial solution. But such swaps raise ethical questions relating to the control of resources in developing countries.

debt-relief may take the form of either refinancing or rescheduling, or cancellation of all repayments. A loan is refinanced when the creditor country makes a new loan to enable the debtor country to meet the debt service payments on an earlier loan. A loan is rescheduled when the amortisation or interest or both on the outstanding portion are rearranged to make payment easier.

debt servicing the sum of interest payments and payments of principal on external debt. The debt service ratio is total debt service divided by exports of goods and services.

devaluation reducing the value of a currency in terms of the monetary metal (e.g. gold) or in terms of another currency. A country with a fundamental disequilibrium in its balance of payments may devalue to stimulate its exports and to discourage imports. It is a remedy which cannot be applied repeatedly without other countries losing confidence in a currency.

economically active population that part of the population which is regularly employed in any sector of the economy and is reflected in standard economic indicators, e.g. GDP and GNP statistics.

fiscal policy the use of taxation through the budget to regulate the aggregate level of economic activity. Thus, if unemployment is regarded as excessive, income and expenditure taxes may be varied to stimulate the level of aggregate demand for this purpose.

foreign direct investment investment by companies, for example transnational corporations, in their foreign subsidiaries.

GDP (gross domestic product) the total final output of foods and services produced by an economy – that is, by residents and non-residents, regardless of the allocation to domestic and foreign claims. It is calculated without making deductions for depreciation.

GNP (gross national product) the total domestic and foreign output claimed by residents. It comprises gross domestic product adjusted by net factor income from abroad. Factor

income comprises receipts that residents receive from abroad for factor services (labour, investment, and interest) less similar payments made to non-residents abroad. It is calculated without making deductions for depreciation.

import regulation can be imposed through tariffs, quotas, restriction of foreign exchange to importers, direct prohibition, import deposits or surcharges. They are usually used to try to correct an adverse balance of payments, or to prohibit goods considered undesirable.

IMR (infant mortality rate) annual deaths of infants under one year of age per 1,000 live births.

inflation happens when the quantity of money is increasing more rapidly than output. Inflation can be caused by (a) government expenditure not covered by taxation or by borrowing, (b) over-stimulation of demand through increases in the money supply, in order to try to maintain high employment levels.

interest charges amounts payable by a borrower for the use of a sum of money for a period of time. Loans to developing countries are sometimes interest-free or carry fixed concessionary rates of interest, as in the case of the UK.

international commodity agreements (ICAs) negotiated under the UN Conference on Trade and Development (UNCTAD) Integrated Programme for Commodities. Those concerning tin, rubber, coffee and cocoa are designed to stabilise prices, at a level both equitable to consumers and fair and remunerative to producers, through the use of buffer stocks and/or export controls. Other ICAs, without economic provisions, are concerned primarily with research and development (jute and tropical timber) or are purely administrative (sugar). The IPC also covers bananas, bauxite, copper, cotton, hard fibres, iron ore, manganese, meat, oils and fats, phosphates, and tea.

interest rate the percentage of the amount borrowed which must be paid annually by the debtor to the creditor, in addition to repayment of capital, to compensate the creditor for the lost use of his money.

letters of credit documents authorising a bank to pay the bearer a specified amount of money; these are used as a means of settlement for foreign trade transactions, the purchaser establishing a credit in favour of his creditor at a bank.

loan loss reserve funds put aside by a bank to cover loans it fears will not be repaid.

moratorium a temporary halt to all payment of interest and principle on a loan.

money supply usually means the total value of bank deposits, on both current account and deposit account, of the commercial banks together with the total amount in cash. Other means of payment are regarded as substitutes for money.

ODA (Official Development Assistance) grants and loans made on concessional financial terms from official sources, with the objective of promoting economic development and welfare. It includes the value of technical cooperation and assistance.

official debt debt owed to public creditors, such as governments, multilateral development banks, such as the World Bank, and the IMF.

own debt purchase taking advantage of discounted rates on the secondary market, a debtor country 'buys back' its own debts. To date, there has been only one example – that of Bolivia. (See **debt-conservation swaps**.)

petrodollars dollars earned from oil sales and deposited in Western banks in the mid-to-late 1970s.

price controls in force when the state either (a) fixes a maximum price in order to protect consumers against high prices, or (b) fixes a minimum price to protect producers against low prices. It is more usual to restrict the term to (a) and designate (b) as price support.

protectionism the imposition of duties and quantitative and other restrictions on imports, in order to 'protect' home producers of those products by making foreign goods dearer.

repudiation the wholesale or selective (of parts which may be considered illegitimate) repudiation of a country's debt. Unlikely to be adopted by many countries because of the inevitable denial of further credit, but selective debt repudiation has been implemented by some countries, e.g. Nigeria with regard to some trade credits advanced to earlier Nigerian administrations. Option favoured by some groups in the Philippines, particularly in relation to some of the debts incurred by the Marcos government.

rescheduling stretching out of repayments, an ongoing method located largely within the framework of crisis management on a case-by-case basis. It has proved unsatisfactory as it seriously underemphasises factors external to the individual debtor, such as terms of trade deterioration, the impact of recession and protectionism in industrialised countries.

secondary debt market fearing total loss, private banks may offer a developing country's debt for sale to other banks at a discount. Such debts may also be acquired by private or public agencies and resold to the debtor government in local currency, e.g. for investment in development or environmental projects.

Stabex the European Community scheme first established under the Lomé Convention to compensate the African, Caribbean and Pacific (ACP) countries for falls in export earnings. Under it, an ACP state receives compensation if earnings from certain commodities fall below reference levels based on previous years' performance. The compensatory payments take the form of loans repayable over the five-year life of the scheme. Countries are expected to make repayment when their commodity earnings rise above a given level. In the case of the 26 poorest ACP countries, no repayment is required. The recipient country is free to decide how to use the resources transferred, informing the Community annually of its actions.

stabilisation an extreme variation of adjustment, in which the emphasis is on 'stabilising' the external and internal deficits in the short term, often by sharp reductions in the level of economic activity. Relatively little weight is given to maintaining or resolving economic growth, which in stabilisation is usually treated as a longer-term issue.

terms of trade the ratio of export prices to import prices, calculated as the unit value of exports over the unit value of imports. An improvement in the terms of trade means that export prices have increased to a greater extent than import prices, or import prices have fallen to a greater extent than export prices; a smaller volume of exports would thus be required to pay for a given volume of imports.

tied and untied aid aid is said to be 'untied' when it is not subject to any geographical limitations on procurement, 'tied' when procurement is limited to the goods and services of the donor country, and 'partially tied' when not wholly exempt from procurement limitations. Assistance is 'double-tied' when it is tied as to both the origin and the nature of the goods or project.

tranche credit granted by IMF to its member nations. Each country is entitled to a series of four tranches under increasingly difficult conditions. The first tranche usually carries few conditions; the fourth might be contingent on stringent economic reforms such as a reduced or eliminated budget deficit.

transnational corporations (TNCs) the official UN term for multinational corporations, usually understood to mean those private corporations with direct investments and production facilities abroad. It does not normally mean those companies whose overseas operations are confined exclusively to sales. The enormous economic power of the TNCs in relation to developing countries, their ability in some cases to dominate local economies and governments, and what the developing countries see as the TNC's one-sided exploitation of their natural resources, have given rise to demands for a code of conduct to govern the activities of TNCs.

write-downs when a bank reduces the default on its loans. Seen as acknowledgement that they have 'gone bad', but largely a book-keeping move; debtor countries are still required to pay in full.

ANNEX II

A GUIDE TO EDUCATION AND ACTION

THIS ANNEX IS INTENDED to provide assistance and material to those who wish to use the book for teaching or discussion purposes. It includes guidance on organising a discussion group, seminar or workshop; a discussion guide; and an agenda for action.

HOW TO ORGANISE A DISCUSSION GROUP, SEMINAR OR WORKSHOP

First Session: Ask the members of the group to introduce themselves briefly, indicating their motivation for joining the group. Test the level of awareness by asking everyone to take a piece of paper and note the six characteristics which first come to mind when they think of the world economic crisis. If possible, show a film, then introduce the topic to the group. Open the floor for discussion, making sure that each expresses his or her expectations from the group meeting. If the group exceeds 10 or 12 persons, subdivide it or ask pairs to exchange ideas for 10 minutes prior to group discussion. Each session should last for approximately 90 minutes. If possible, invite a resource person to address this and/or the final sessions.

Subsequent Sessions: Taking the various subjects headlined in the book, introduce the topic to the group or ask someone who is well-prepared to do so. Guide the discussion on the basis of the questions included at the end of each chapter. Do not hesitate to make up your own questions. Where relevant, the group could use 20 minutes for preparing a role-play on the topic, using the case studies included in the book.

Final Session: Discuss a possible plan of action for your community. Identify the field in which your group desires to work. Invite representatives of those services which may be prepared to cooperate (e.g. local authorities, representatives of local health, education and social services, or of voluntary or official aid agencies). Identify short-term and long-range goals. Ensure that each member of the group understands his/her possibilities for action. Set a date for the first progress report.

HOW TO USE THE BOOK FOR A SEMINAR OR WORKSHOP

The schedule overleaf presupposes a minimum of five days and a group not exceeding 35 participants. Should there be more or less time, or a different number of participants, the programme can be modified, e.g. a workshop to take place at the local level can be spread over several weeks, with one-day or evening sessions dealing with specific aspects and topics.

Those who plan the seminar, and group leaders, should be well-chosen, well prepared for their tasks and should get to know each other, their backgrounds and their main interests. They should discuss the different aspects of the subject in order to clarify issues and concepts, as well as controversial points which might slow down the process. Responsibility for each aspect of the preparatory work should be defined, including plans for evaluation and follow-up. Procedures on the lines of those suggested for discussion groups should be followed.

Ask participants to list situations which can be considered relevant, and invite them to prepare posters giving succinct and effective messages to the general public. Inviting talented participants to chair a session contributes to their leadership development, but the chairing of the last session, including summing-up, presentation and adoption of recommendations, should be by an experienced person.

SUGGESTED CHECK-LIST FOR THE PREPARATORY MEETING

- Introduction of participants.
- General debate on the subject; clarification of issues and concepts.
- Target groups to be reached.
- Criteria upon which participants should be selected.
- Identification of resource persons.
- Cooperation with other local and international groups.
- Language(s) in which the seminar will

be conducted.

- Decisions on place and date of seminar, and registration fee.
- Organisation of schedule (see attached) and method of work.
- Responsibility for each aspect of preparatory work to be clearly defined; selection of preparatory and homework materials.
- Decisions concerning distribution of programme announcements (six weeks prior to the event, through co-sponsoring groups).
- Design of evaluation sheet to be distributed to participants.
- Plans for follow-up activities.

PLAN FOR A SEMINAR

	First day	Second day	Third day	Fourth day	Fifth day
09.00–10.30	–	Introduction to the subject – lecture and plenary discussion	Speaker on: *Employment health and social services issues*	*Responses to the crisis –* panel, and plenary discussion	Presentation of plans for action to plenary – discussion
10.30–11.00 (*coffee/tea*)	–				
11.00–12.30	–	*Origins and mechanisms of the crisis –* panel and plenary discussion	3 Working groups on above topics – written reports	Working group: (1) *Policy responses; (2) Grassroots*	Presentation and adoption of recommendations– plenary, written reports
12.30 (*lunch*)	–				
14.30	Arrival of participants, registration	*Impact of structural adjustment on women–* lecture and plenary discussion	*Consequences for women as citizens –* panel and plenary discussion	*Development education agenda –* working groups, written reports	(continue if necessary) Closure of seminar
16.30–17.00 (*coffee/tea*)	–				
17.00	Welcoming addresses, introduction of participants	Working groups on above topics – written reports	Working group on above topic – written reports	Presentation of working group reports to plenary	
18.30	Introduction to the seminar – films	(continued)	(continued)	Plenary discussion	
19.30 (*dinner*)					

DISCUSSION GUIDE

The following questions, which relate to the different chapters, are of varying degrees of difficulty; discussion leaders can either choose among them, depending upon the age and state of knowledge of the group, or provide questions of their own.

CHAPTER 1 ────────────────────

1. Why has the fairly steady progress in

developing countries which took place in the 1970s been reversed during the 1980s? Was this reversal due to a sudden deterioration in the internal policies of developing countries, or to adverse changes in the world economy?

2. What was the effect on developing countries of the steep rise in oil prices (a) in 1973, and (b) 1978–79? Why has the unprecedented fall in other commodity prices been such a shock to developing countries? What has caused it?

3. Can you account for rising protectionism in the industrialised countries? What is its effect on developing countries' exports?

4. Why did world interest rates rise at such a phenomenal rate in the early 1980s? What did this mean (a) for creditor nations, (b) for debtor nations, (c) for the banks?

5. Which multilateral institution is the lending agency 'of last resort'? Can you name some of its conditions for lending funds to indebted countries?

6. Would you say that there is a broad consensus that debt reduction and changes in international trading patterns could and should play an important role in adjustment strategies?

7. To what extent have military expenditures contributed to the world economic crisis?

8. How have prior national policies towards women aggravated the effects of the economic crisis upon them?

CHAPTER 2 ————————————

1. Why, when we speak of the 'poorest of the poor', do we almost always mean women?

2. What has been the effect in developing countries of adjustment policies on (a) food prices and availability, (b) employment, (c) the basic wage structure? What form does women's work usually take in the export-processing zones? What do we mean by the 'informal sector'?

3. For what reasons is it said that micro-level income-generating programmes for women have often, inadvertently, reinforced women's marginalisation from the wider economic process?

4. Why should short-term reduction of government and local expenditures on health and education lead to a long-term result, i.e. permanent damage to the physical and mental capacity of the future labour force?

5. How are women's roles as health-care providers and educators in developing countries affected by the world economic crisis and adjustment policies? Why are they the 'first victims'?

6. What do sharp increases in food prices and reduction of food subsidies have to do with the world economic crisis? What is the relationship between them and growing poverty in developing countries?

7. How are households trying to increase their income-earning potential or reduce living costs? Why have women in many cases become the sole supporters of rural households? How does this affect their need for, and access to, land and credit?

8. What has been the effect of the world economic crisis, and growing poverty, on families in industrialised countries? What is the extent of homelessness and unemployment in countries such as the United States? Why have average earnings and educational standards dropped in that country?

9. Can you name the most wretched group among the hungry homeless in the United States? Why are they a cheap source of labour?

10. Health and education professions are fighting to maintain and expand government programmes for the poor, even during a period of economic adjustment in the US. Why is the US, considered the richest country in the world until it too became heavily indebted, undertaking an economic adjustment programme? Is this being undertaken in collaboration with the IMF?

11. Explain how conditions which make women the first to lose their jobs in times of high unemployment, and require them to spend more time caring for their families in the absence of adequate social services, can affect women's role as citizens.

12. How important is it, to women, to their families and to their communities, that they play a major role in local activities, labour unions, trade associations and economic institutions? In other words, how important is women's participation in development?

13. Implementation of CEDAW (the UN Convention on the Elimination of all Forms of Discrimination against Women) depends largely upon public monitoring in those states which have ratified the Convention. What role can women play in this respect?

14. Do you consider that women should be involved in the design of structural adjustment packages, since they are key figures in the process?

15. What do the following 'unrecognised issues' have to do with the world economic crisis: unpaid work, increased violence, sexual harassment, prostitution?

16. What role has discrimination against women played in precipitating the world economic crisis? If their role in society and in development had been recognised a decade ago, do you think we should still have had a world economic crisis? If so, why; if not, why not?

CHAPTER 3

1. What are the major elements of the human-face adjustment strategies proposed by UNICEF? Which of them are designed to increase the productivity of small farmers? Can day-care centres make a difference to rural women? How useful are public works schemes and food-for-work programmes?

2. Can compensatory programmes help to avoid the negative effects of macro-economic adjustment programmes? If so, which do you consider the most useful: income-generation, income-transfer, food supplement, price subsidy, nutrition education, primary health care?

3. Can health-care be improved by health education and social mobilisation? In what spheres can such social mobilisation best be accomplished? Should the school system be used as a centre of community action, thus strengthening its wider social and development role? Should female participation in the school system be encouraged as a way of giving them more decision-making power in the community?

4. What, in your view, should be the most important aspects of IMF structural adjustment programmes in developing countries, and of World Bank development activities?

CHAPTER 4

1. The European Conference of Parliamentarians and NGOs on North-South Interdependence and Solidarity considered

that, for the poorest countries, debt should be cancelled or 'forgiven' and the finance recouped used to create jobs for women. Would this (a) beggar the banks, (b) contribute to development, (c) be a suitable way to increase employment for women?

2. Other suggestions include default, setting a debt ceiling, creating a debtors' cartel, increased South-South trade, conversion of debts into gifts, partial non-repayment or postponement of repayment, repayment in proportion to export revenues, conversions and swaps, linkage of repayment to former prices, and the return of flight capital. Do you think any of these are the answer to the problem?

3. Some commentators believe that more bank lending could only prolong the debt crisis, and that a durable solution should address the real economic aspects of the present world order, North-South inequality in trade, and unjust social structures that create and maintain poverty. What is your opinion?

4. Why do NGOs lay such stress on the need for increased responsibility of commercial banks for the social effects of their loans to Third World countries? What was the banks' original purpose in lending?

CHAPTER 5

1. Anita Anand has said that the success stories of the decade are the micro-efforts. What does she mean by this?

2. UNIFEM's revolving loan funds are helping many women at the local level to be more economically independent. In Swaziland, why is this tied to the skills training project? What is meant by the term 'revolving'?

3. Why do special banks for the rural poor, such as the Grameen Bank in Bangladesh and the SEWA Bank in India,

make such a big contribution to the emancipation of women and their contribution to the development effort?

4. Why is credit so important to women, and the availability of capital so important to self-reliance programmes? Would availability of credit make it easier for rural women to cope with double-cropping?

5. Do you think the Bolivian Mothers Clubs used food aid provided by the World Food Programme in a suitable way? Should other forms of 'aid-in-kind' be used in this manner?

6. Training centres for local and provincial women normally offer courses in nutrition, health, appropriate technology, textiles, basketwork, etc. Should they also offer small business and credit management, sales, book-keeping, etc. to encourage women to become entrepreneurs?

CHAPTER 6

1. What have been the effects of: (a) inflation, (b) devaluation of its currency, and (c) the steep fall in commodity prices, on the Zambian economy? Why is the price of copper so important to Zambia?

2. Did the IMF's suggestion to auction the Zambian currency help to control inflation and to meet Zambia's debt problem?

3. What were the reasons for Zambia's break with the International Monetary Fund and the World Bank? What were the consequences?

4. What have been the consequences of the drastic cuts in social services, such as health and education? What have been the effects on women?

5. Will Zambia's economic recovery programme, with renewed help from IMF and the World Bank, help to solve debt and adjustment problems? Will it encour-

age greater assistance to women?

6. Do you think stone-crushing on the highway is an appropriate task for a woman? If not, why do you think the women of Lusaka engage in such an activity, even with babies on their backs?

CHAPTER 7

1. What has been the effect on women in agriculture of increasing migration of rural workers to the cities, or to other countries?

2. We speak of women's domestic and agricultural labour as unpaid and unrecognised labour. Why?

3. In Mexico, in addition to growing participation of women in paid agricultural labour, a new area of paid work has emerged: the 'putting out' system. What does this mean? Do you consider it likely to lead to greater exploitation of women's labour?

4. Have export-oriented policies and the rural exodus affected the real wages and conditions of employment of women in urban areas?

CHAPTER 8

1. After posting real GNP growth rates averaging 6% in the 1970s, in 1984 the Philippines' debt stood at $27 billion and inflation was at 64%. Filipinos give two reasons for the deterioration. What are they?

2. What has been the result of export-oriented policies with regard to women workers (a) in Export Processing Zones; (b) who have taken jobs abroad, or (c) have become active in the 'informal' economy?

3. What are the working, wage and social conditions faced by Filipina overseas contract workers? What steps has the Philippine government taken to try to counteract these conditions?

4. Name three specialised programmes in the Philippines intended to reduce the female unemployment rate, create income-generating opportunities for women, and provide them with equal opportunities.

5. What is your opinion with regard to the social unrest and rioting that has occurred in protest against economic adjustment policies?

CHAPTER 9

1. Ghana has been one of the countries most seriously affected by the world economic crisis. Why did mineral and cocoa production fall so precipitously between 1975 and 1982, followed by a sharp fall in the price of cocoa? What effect did this have on the volume of imports?

2. What other, natural, disaster in 1982 aggravated the situation and caused the worst food shortages since Ghana gained independence? Why did one million Ghanaians return suddenly from Nigeria in 1983?

3. How has the crisis affected Ghanaian households? Examine the effect upon (a) real incomes, (b) food prices, (c) employment. How many families now fall below the absolute poverty line estimated by the World Bank?

4. What has been the effect of the crisis upon the health sector in Ghana, for example with regard to hospital and clinic equipment, basic drugs, and access of the population to primary health care? What is the situation with regard to communicable diseases, malnutrition and maternal and child health?

5. How have foreign exchange shortages affected the education sector in Ghana? What is the reason for the exodus of trained teachers? How is the deterioration in the education system linked to high

drop-out rates and child labour, especially among girls?

6. Which are the categories most acutely affected by the economic crisis (a) in urban centres, (b) in rural areas, (c) within households?

7. In which ways does the Ghanaian government's Economic Recovery Programme try to rehabilitate the human dimension of the economy? Has its programme achieved significant popular support?

8. Have a decrease in the inflation rate and improvements in cocoa production been reflected in improvements in human welfare in Ghana? If not, what policies can be considered top priorities to protect and improve the conditions of vulnerable groups?

CHAPTER 10

1. In Jamaica, debt servicing has risen from 26% of total expenditure in 1982–83 to 42% in 1985–86. What effect has this had on social services in the island, i.e. health care, nutrition, educational facilities?

2. What is meant by a devaluation of the currency?

3. Why are there so many (some 33%) female-headed households in Jamaica? yet women constitute 46% of the labour force. Does this make it a matriarchal society? What can be done to enable mothers both to care for their children and earn a living for the family?

4. Who are the 'higglers'? What is the value of the contribution they, and other women working in the informal sector, make to the Jamaican economy?

5. Why are employment opportunities for women in the Export-Free Zone under such heavy attack in Jamaica?

6. Why has the crisis had such an impact

upon Jamaica's adult literacy programme?

7. Does Jamaica have a National Health Care Programme?

CHAPTER 11

1. 'Iusticia et Pax' has proposed the concept of co-responsibility for both the causes and the solutions relative to international debt, in the interests of solidarity. In what sense do you see a shared responsibility between industrialised nations and developing countries in this respect, and how do you interpret the term solidarity?

2. Do you believe that the industrialised countries bear the heavier responsibility, even if the economic crisis has also faced them with grave problems of reconversion and unemployment? If so, how can they meet that responsibility?

3. If the responsibility for informing and educating the public with regard to the duties of extended solidarity falls upon social, economic, educational and religious leaders and especially upon politicians, how well do you consider this responsibility is being met, in both North and South? Do you consider that the media (press, radio, TV) do enough to explain the world economic crisis and the debt issue?

4. It has been suggested that adopting specific measures to relaunch growth, reduced protectionism, lower interest rates and assign a just value to raw materials lies within the purview of the industrialised societies. Do you see these as measures which are likely to be adopted by governments only in response to public pressure?

5. Proposals made at the UN/NGO Workshop in Oxford were intended to strengthen NGOs involved in education and campaigning, research and training, and/or operational work. How can non-

governmental organisations carry out this work, and how can individuals contribute to it?

6. Why do NGOs lay such stress on the need for increased responsibility of commercial banks for the social effects of their loans to Third World countries? What was their original purpose in lending this money?

7. To what extent do corruption and capital flight explain the world economic crisis, and what can be done about them?

8. How has your family, your community, your nation been affected by the debt situation and the economic crisis? Has it affected your own education, or hopes for a career?

9. What is the general feeling in your community about 'aid' to developing countries and the 'homeless and hungry poor'? How do you feel about the failure of industrialised countries to keep their promise to devote a minimum of 0.7% of their GNP to this purpose?

10. Women's organisations in Bolivia have been vocal and often militant in their protests about the social costs of their country's debt. Do you think they should be able to count on the support of women's organisations in the North? Do you think War on Want's campaign with bank users in Britain will be an effective contribution in this respect?

11. The need for relevant data on the social impact of adjustment programmes is recognised. Should this be undertaken by national institutions or by women's organisations and others working at grass-roots level? How important are women's literacy programmes in this regard?

12. What do the members of the WAES network mean by economic literacy and a 'women's alternative economic summit'?

ACTION AGENDA

Informed citizens willing to work on the local and national levels to increase awareness of debt and adjustment problems and of their impact on women, and of the need to take emergency action at these levels as well as at the global level, can make a considerable contribution to the resolution of those problems. Some of the suggestions which follow may be more relevant to groups in industrialised countries than to developing countries, to urban rather than to rural areas. Choose those that are most appropriate for your circumstances. Remember that effective action by women's and development groups at the national and global levels requires, in the first place, action at the local level. And that every voice, every action, can make a difference.

1. Inform yourself: Having absorbed the information in this book, read further in the publications listed in the Bibliography and ask for information and advice from the organisations listed in Annex III.

2. Invite a specialist in the subject to address your group: invite a local official to speak about poverty in your community, the services and programmes available for the hungry and homeless, and local government plans to improve the situation. Compile information about special services for the poorest of the poor, and make this available to the public through production of information materials; ask the media to publicise it.

3. Undertake research with regard to poor women, both locally and nationally; collect data concerning numbers involved and the causes and consequences of this poverty. Write about the results of your research in the local newspaper, or speak about them on local radio. Combine your efforts with others for greater impact.

4. Investigate the effect upon employment

in your country of the economic crisis, and its particular repercussions upon women. Compare the situation as it affects men and women, and its impact upon child labour.

5. Check government expenditures on arms and defence in relation to expenditures on health and education.

6. Visit a local clinic to see conditions for yourself. Ask about the facilities, availability of drugs, and conditions in which sick people are cared for. Investigate the health record of a typical health establishment, and the application of primary health care measures.

7. Check nutrition statistics in your community, and information upon malnutrition's direct effect upon pregnant women and children. Find out whether any special care is taken with regard to these vulnerable groups, for example with food supplements, food stamps, food-for-work programmes.

8. Check education enrolment. Find out whether all children of school age are in fact at school, and whether there is a difference between boy and girl attendance. Ask what the local and national authorities are doing to improve educational facilities and their availability to girls, and to women in adult education.

9. As a group, discuss (using the discussion guide) what you can do to (a) alleviate the situation directly, (b) undertake an information and education campaign to encourage authorities to take action, (c) encourage the media and other institutions in the community to devote more attention to the effects of the world economic crisis on the women of the area.

10. Prepare posters and leaflets for both local and national meetings. Undertake mailbox distribution of informational

leaflets on the subject, inviting recipients to join in your efforts.

11. Initiate neighbourhood discussions on women and poverty in your own community and in a community in the South (or North). Discuss the relationship of this poverty to the world economic crisis. Invite poor women and NGO specialists in the subject as resource persons.

12. Ask your local parliamentary representative to raise a question with the government concerning its attitude to indebtedness, its own or that of creditor nations. Invite him or her to speak on the subject at a local workshop. Invite a homeless woman as resource person.

13. Organise meetings at which international and national specialists will speak about the impact of external economic conditions on a country's trade and development.

14. Encourage development education in schools, and offer posters and educational materials for use in the classroom. Invite teachers and parents to join your group, or to participate in your campaigns for greater justice for 'the poorest of the poor'. Promote peace education in schools, emphasising the discrepancy between the billions of dollars spent on armaments and the amount available for social services.

15. Research the numbers and particular reponsibilities of women in your Foreign Ministry and your UN Delegation. Ask them for a statement on the world economic crisis and its effect upon women in your country, and upon women in the South (or North). Invite them to speak at a meeting or workshop.

16. Participate in NGO campaigns urging governments to take action to reduce or cancel debt repayments, to give higher priority to development assistance, and

to take positive measures at the international level to improve global trading conditions.

17. In collaboration with other groups and non-governmental agencies, organise a national conference at which Ministers for Trade and Development, Health and Social Services will discuss the situation both nationally and internationally. Ask a UN specialist to be the keynote speaker.

18. Work towards improvement in the status of women, emphasising that discrimination against women becomes a double-edged weapon in times of economic recession. Link up with an international network of women attempting to bring feminine concepts and perspectives into discussions concerning debt and development.

ANNEX III

LIST OF

ORGANISATIONS

INTERNATIONAL AND INTERGOVERNMENTAL

Council of Europe, BP 431 R6, 67006, Strasbourg Cedex, France.

European Economic Community, rue de la Loi, B-1049 Brussels, Belgium.

International Research and Training Institute for the Advancement of Women (INSTRAW), Santo Domingo, Dominican Republic.

International Fund for Agricultural Development (IFAD), 107 via del Serafico, 00142 Rome.

International Labour Office (ILO), 4 route des Morillons, 1211 Geneva.

International Monetary Fund, 700 19th Street N.W., Washington DC 20431.

OECD Development Centre, 94 rue Chardon-Lagache, 75016 Paris.

United Nations Centre for Social Development and Humanitarian Affairs (UNOV/CSDHA), Division for the Advancement of Women, Vienna International Centre, PO Box 500, A-1400 Vienna, Austria.

United Nations Conference on Trade and Development (UNCTAD), Palais des Nations, 1211 Geneva 10.

United Nations Development Programme (UNDP), 1 United Nations Plaza, New York, NY 10017; *also* Palais des Nations, Geneva.

United Nations Development Fund for Women (UNIFEM), c/o UNDP, NY.

United Nations High Commissioner for Refugees (UNHCR), Centre William Rappard, 154 rue de Lausanne, 1202 Geneva.

United Nations Non-Governmental Liaison Service, United Nations, Geneva and New York.

UNICEF, 3 United Nations Plaza, New York NY 10017; also Palais des Nations, Geneva.

United Nations Office at Geneva, Palais des Nations, 1211 Geneva 10.

World Bank, 1818 H Street, NW, Washington DC 20433; *also* 66, Avenue d'Iéna, F.75116, Paris.

World Food Programme, via delle Terme di Caracalla, I-00100 Rome.

World Health Organisation, Avenue Appia 20, 1202 Geneva.

INTERNATIONAL NGOS

ACORD, Francis House, Francis Street, London SW1P 1DQ.

Asian and Pacific Development Centre (APDC), Kuala Lumpur, Malaysia.

Association of African Women for Research and Development (AAWORD), c/o CODESRIA, BP 3304, Dakar, Senegal.

Commission on the Churches' Participation in Development (CCPD), World Council of Churches, 150 Route de Ferney, 1211 Geneva 20.

Development Alternatives with Women for a New Era (DAWN), APDEC, Pesiaran Duta, PO Box 12224, Kuala Lumpur, Malaysia.

Debt Crisis Network, 1901 Q St., NW, Washington DC 20009.

Depthnews Women's Feature Service, PO Box 1843 Manila, Philippines.

Environment Liaison Centre (ELC), PO Box 72461 Nairobi, Kenya.

Interfaith Action for Economic Justice, 110 Maryland Avenue, NE, Washington DC 20002.

International Alliance of Women, Alemannengasse 42, CH-4058 Basel.

International Centre for Research on Women, 1717 Massachusetts Avenue N.W., Suite 501, Washington DC 20036.

International Coalition for Development Action (ICDA), 22 rue des Bollandistes, 1040 Brussels, Belgium.

International Confederation of Free Trade Unions (ICFTU), c/o Trade Union Congress, 23–28 Gt. Russell St., London WC1B 3LS.

International Cooperation for Development and

Solidarity (CIDSE), 1 Ave. des Arts, Boîte 6, B-1040 Brussels, Belgium.

International Council of Jewish Women, 19 rue de Teheran, 75008, Paris.

International Council of Voluntary Agencies (ICVA), 13 rue Gautier, 1201 Geneva.

International Council of Women, 13 rue Caumartin, 75009 Paris.

International Council on Social Welfare, Koestlergasse 1/29, A-1060 Vienna.

International Federation of University Women, 37 Quai Wilson, 1201 Geneva.

International Federation of Women in Legal Careers, 6, via R. Giovagnoli, 00152 Rome.

International Women's Tribune Centre, 777 UN Plaza, New York 10017.

International Organisation of Consumer Unions, POB 1045, 10830 Penang, Malaysia.

ISIS/WICCE Women's International Cross-Cultural Exchange, 29 rue des Gares, 1201 Geneva.

Lutheran World Federation, 150 Route de Ferney, 1211 Geneva 20.

Medical Women's International Association, Herbert-Lewin-Strasse 5, D-5000 Cologne 41, Fed.Rep.of Germany.

Third World Network, 87 Cantonment Road, 10250 Penang, Malaysia.

Women's International League for Peace and Freedom, 1 rue de Varembé, 1211 Geneva 20.

World Association of Girl Guides and Girl Scouts, 12c Lyndhurst Road, London NW3 5PQ.

World Association for the School as an Instrument of Peace, 5, rue du Simplon, 1207 Geneva.

World Federation of Methodist Women, 777 UN Plaza, New York NY 10017.

World Union of Catholic Women's Organisations, 20 rue Notre-Dame des Champs, 75006 Paris.

Youth for Development and Cooperation (YDC), 21 Leiliegracht, 1016 GR Amsterdam.

Zonta International, 557 West Randolph Street, Chicago Ill. 60606-2284, USA.

NATIONAL (GOVERNMENTAL AND NGO)

AUSTRALIA Australian Council for Overseas Aid (ACFOA), GPO Box 1562, Canberra.

International Women's Development Agency, 139 Hoddle St., Richmond, Vic. 3121, Australia.

BANGLADESH Bangladesh Institute for Development Studies, 17/E Agargaon, Dhaka.

BELGIUM National Centre for Development Cooperation (NCOS), 76 rue de Laeken, 1000 Brussels.

BRAZIL Ibase, Instituto Bresileiro de Analises Sociaise Economicas, 155 Av. Nilo Pecanha, 20020 Rio de Janeiro.

CANADA Canadian International Development Agency (CIDA), 200 Promenade du Portage, Hull, Quebec, Canada K1A 0G4.

Canadian Council for International Cooperation, One Nicholas Street, Ottawa.

DENMARK Danish International Development Agency (DANIDA), Asiatisk Plats 2, DK-1448, Copenhagen.

FINLAND Finnish International Development Agency (FINNIDA), POB 276, 00171 Helsinki.

Finnish United Nations Association, Unioninkatu 45 B, SF-00170, Helsinki

FRANCE Centre de recherche et d'information pour le développement (CRID), 49 rue de la Glacière, 75013 Paris.

INDIA All-India Women's Conference, Sarojini House, 6 Bhawandas Road, New Delhi.

IRELAND Trocaire, 169 Booterstown Avenue, Blackrock, Co. Dublin.

NETHERLANDS Forum on Debt and Development (FONDAD), Noordeinde 107A. 2514 GE, The Hague.

Netherlands Organisation for International Development (NOVIB), Amaliastraat 7, 2514 JC The Hague.

NORWAY NIEO Network, St. Olavsgt. 29, N-0166 Oslo.

Norwegian Agency for Development (NORAD), POB 8142, Dep. 0033 Oslo 1.

PERU DESCO (Centro de estudios y promociòn del desarollo), 110 Leon de la Fuente, Lima 17.

PHILIPPINES Depthnews, POB 1843, Manila.

Freedom from Debt Coalition, University of the Philippines, Room 301, Alumni Center,

Quezon City, 978226 Philippines.

IBON Data Bank, P.O. Box S-447, Sta. Mesa, Manila.

SWEDEN Development Forum of the Swedish Churches, Gotgatan 3 NB, S-75222, Uppsala.

Swedish International Development Agency (SIDA), Birger Jarlsgatan 61, S-10525 Stockholm.

SWITZERLAND Third World Information Service (i3w), Monbijoustrasse 31, Berne.

UGANDA The Grail, P.O. Box 14267, Kampala.

UNITED KINGDOM Catholic Fund for Overseas Development (CAFOD), 2, Garden Close, Stockwell Road, London SW9 9TY.

Catholic Institute for International Relations (CIIR), 22 Coleman Fields, London N1 7AF.

Institute for Development Studies, University of Sussex, UK.

Minority Rights Group, 29 Craven Street, London WC2N 5NT.

Overseas Development Institute, Regent's College, Inner Circle, Regent's Park, London NW1 4NS.

Oxfam, 274 Banbury Road, Oxford OX2 7DZ.

War on Want, 37–39 Great Guildford Street, London SE1 9BT.

World Development Movement (WDM), Bedford Chambers, Covent Garden, London WC2E 8HA.

UNITED STATES OF AMERICA Association for Women in Development, 2607 North 24th Street, Arlington Va. 22207.

Bread for the World, 802 Rhode Island Ave. NE, Washington DC 20018.

Coalition for Women in International Development, 1815 H. Street NW, Washington DC 20433.

InterAction, 200 Park Ave. South, Suite 1114, New York, NY 10003.

Interfaith Action for Economic Justice, 110 Maryland Ave. NE, Washington DC 20002.

Overseas Development Council, 1717 Massachussetts Ave. NW, Suite 501, Washington DC 20036.

The Development Gap, 1400 Eye Street, NW, Suite 520, Washington, DC 20005.

US Agency for International Development (USAID), 320 21st St. N.W., Washington DC 20523.

US Debt Crisis Network, 1400 Eye St. NW, Suite 520, Washington DC 20005.

Women's Foreign Policy Council, 1133 Broadway, New York, NY 10010.

World Development Journal, 1717 Mass. Ave. NW, Washington DC 20036.

Information on women and development issues may also be obtained from or through National Committees for UNICEF or National United Nations Associations.

SELECTIVE BIBLIOGRAPHY

Addison, T. and L. Demery (1985), 'Macro-economic stabilisation, income distribution and poverty: a preliminary survey.' Working Paper 15, Overseas Development Institute, London.

Ahooja-Patel, K. (1985), 'The Place of Women in International Economic Relations,' in G. Ashworth (ed.), *Women's Studies International*.

Allison, C. (1985), 'Women, Land, Labour and Survival: Getting some basic facts straight', *IDS Bulletin*, Sussex.

Allison, H. (1987), 'Challenging the Debt Crisis', *Spare Rib*, No. 176, March 1987. *Also*: (1988), 'The International Debt Crisis – Women the Hardest Hit', *Women's World* No. 17, March 1988, ISIS/WICCE, PO Box 2471, Geneva 2.

Anand, A. (1988), 'Development in the 1990s: Repetition or Innovation?' *Development Forum*, Sept.–Oct. 1988, United Nations, New York.

Anker, R. (1983), 'Female Labour Force Participation in Developing Countries: a critique of current definitions and data collection methods', *International Labour Review* 122 (No. 6), ILO Geneva.

Bell, D.E. and Reich, M.R. (eds.), *Health, Nutrition and Economic Crises: Approaches to policy in the Third World*, Auburn House, Auburn MA, USA, 1988.

Boserup, E. (1970), *Women's Role in Economic Development*, Allen and Unwin, London.

Brandt Commission (1983), *Common Crisis, North-South: Cooperation for Recovery*, Pan Books, London.

CHANGE (1987), *The Cost of Debt: Women and the International Debt Crisis*. P.O. Box 824, London SE24 9JS.

CIDSE (1988), *Third World Debt*. International Cooperation for Development and Solidarity, 1–2 Ave. des Arts, Bte. 6, 1040 Brussels.

Clark, John with David Keen, *Debt and Poverty: a Case Study of Zambia*. OXFAM/UK, May 1988.

Clavano, N.R. (1981), 'International Debt: Analysis, Experience and Prospects', *Journal of Development Planning*, United Nations New York.

Colclough, C., R. Herbold Green, eds. (1988), 'Stabilisation – For Growth or Decay?' *IDS Bulletin*, Jan. 1988, Vol. 19 No. 1, Institute of Development Studies, Sussex.

Coote, Belinda (1985), 'A Case Study of Jamaica', *Debt and Poverty*, OXFAM Public Affairs Unit, Oxford, May 1985.

Cornia, G.A. (1987), 'Economic Decline and Human Welfare in the First Half of the Eighties'. *Also:* 'Adjustment Policies 1980–1985: Effects on Child Welfare'. UNICEF, *Adjustment with a Human Face*, Clarendon Press, Oxford.

Cornia, G.A., R. Jolly, F. Stewart, eds., (1987), *Adjustment with a Human Face*, UNICEF, Clarendon Press, Oxford.

Cornia, G.A. and Clark J. (1987), 'The Adjustment Stalemate: Conventional Approaches and New Ideas; and NGOs and Structural Adjustment', Occasional Paper No. 3, UN/NGLS, Geneva.

Debt Crisis Network, *From Debt to Development: Alternatives to the International Debt Crisis*, Washington D.C. Also: *A Journey through the Global Debt Crisis*, a cartoon book, available from the Institute for Policy Studies/Transnational Institute, 1901 Q St. NW, Washington, DC 20009.

Dell, S. (1986), 'The World Debt Problem: a Diagnosis', Report to the Group of Twenty-four (mimeographed), New York. United Nations Institute for Training and Research.

Diejomach, V.P. 'IMF-assisted Stabilisation and Adjustment Programmes in African Countries: Some Unresolved Issues'. Paper presented to ILO Meeting on Stabilisation and Adjustment Policies. ILO Geneva

1986.

Economic Commission for Latin America and the Caribbean. *Debt, Adjustment and Renegotiation in Latin America: Orthodox and Alternative Approaches,* Reiner (USA) and United Nations (Santiago de Chile), 1986.

Euro-Latin American Conference of NGOs, Lima, Peru, 25–29 January 1988. *The External Debt, Development and International Cooperation,* Ed. L'Harmattan, Paris, 1989.

George, S. (1988), *A Fate Worse than Debt: The World Financial Crisis and the Poor.* Grove Press Inc., 920 Broadway, New York, NY 10010, and Penguin, London.

Gidwani, S. (1985), 'Impact of Monetary and Financial Policies on Women', INSTRAW, *Study on the Role of Women in International Economic Relations,* Santo Domingo.

Godfrey, M. (1985). 'Trade and Exchange Rate Policy: a Further Contribution to the Debate', in Rose, T. (ed.), *Crisis and Recovery in Sub-Saharan Africa,* OECD Paris.

Goldstein, M. (1986), 'The Global Effects of Fund-Supported Adjustment Programmes', Occasional Paper No. 42 IMF, Washington DC.

Green, R.H. (1986), 'Hunger, Poverty and Food Aid in Sub-Saharan Africa', Occasional Paper No. 6, World Food Programme, Rome, 21 July 1986.

Griffin, K. (1988), 'Toward a Cooperative Settlement of the Debt Problem', *Finance and Development,* IMF/World Bank Publications, Washington.

Griffith-Jones, S. and O. Sunkel (1988), *Debt and Development Crises in Latin America: The End of an Illusion.* Oxford University Press, Oxford.

Hay, R.W. (1986), 'Food Aid and Relief – Development Strategies', Occasional Paper No. 8, World Food Programme, Rome, 23 July 1986.

Heyzer, N., ed., (1987), *Women Farmers and Rural Change in Asia: Towards Equal Access and Participation.* Also ed. (1988), *Daughters in Industry: Work Skills and Consciousness of Women Workers in Asia.* Asian and Pacific Development Centre, Kuala Lumpur, Malaysia.

Hicks, N., and A. Kubisch (1983), 'The Effects of Expenditure Reduction in Developing Countries' (mimeographed), World Bank, Washington DC.

Hoeven, R. van der (1987), 'External Shocks and Stabilisation Policies: Spreading the Load', *International Labour Review,* Vol. 26, No. 2.

Hossain, M. (1984), 'Impact of the Grameen Bank on Women's Involvement in Productive Activities'. Paper presented at UN/ESCAP Workshop on 'Bank Credit for Landless Women'. Dhaka, Bangladesh.

International Fund for Agricultural Development 'Hunger amidst Food Surpluses: the IFAD View'. Intro. to *IFAD Annual Report,* Rome, 1986.

International Labour Organisation. *Labour and Society,* Vol. II, No. 3. Includes articles by then-US Treasury Secretary James Baker, the IMF and A.W. Clausen, with case studies of individual countries which have recently implemented IMF and World Bank policies, and bibliography. French/English. ILO Geneva, 1986; *Also:* ILO Working document (No. 1) and Background document (No. 2) for High-Level Meeting on Employment and Structural Adjustment, 23–25 November 1987. International Labour Organisation, Geneva; *Also:* ILO, Asian Employment Programme. *Structural Adjustment: By Whom, For Whom?* ILO New Delhi, 1987; *Also:* see under World Employment Programme (WEP).

International Monetary Fund and World Bank (1987), *Finance and Development,* Vol. 24, No. 1, on capital flight, external debt and adjustment programmes. Washington DC, March 1987. *Also:* Vol. 24, No. 2, on adjustment and growth. Washington DC, June 1987.

Islam Rahman, R. (1986), 'The Impact of

Grameen Bank on the Situation of Poor Rural Women', Working Paper 1, Grameen Evaluation Project, Bangladesh Institute of Development Studies.

Ivan-Smith, E., N. Tandon, J. Connors, *Women in Sub-Saharan Africa*, Minority Rights Group, 29 Craven Street, London WC2N 5NT.

Joekes, S. (1987), *Women in the World Economy: an INSTRAW Study*, Oxford University Press.

Johnstone, V. (1987), 'Rural Women Plan for Income and Community Development', International Women's Development Agency Report No. 7, Australia.

Jolly, R. (1987), 'Women's Needs and Adjustment Policies in Developing Countries', UNDP Roundtable on Managing Human Development, Budapest, 6–9 September 1987.

Jolly, R. and Cornia, G.A. (eds.), (1984), *Impact of the World Recession on Children* (Prepared for UNICEF). Pergamon Press, Oxford.

Khan, M.S. and M.D. Knight (1985), 'Fund-supported Programmes and Economic Growth', Occasional Paper 41, IMF, Washington DC.

Killick, T., ed. (1984), *The Quest for Economic Stabilisation: the IMF and the Third World*. Heinemann, London; also (1985), 'Developing Countries and the Changing International Financial Environment', Paper prepared for ILO meeting in January 1986.

Kunanayakam, T. (1988), 'The Debt Crisis and Development Disaster', DEF- *Development Education Forum*, November 1988, Lutheran World Federation, PO Box 66, 1211 Geneva 20.

Lele, U. (1986), 'Women and Structural Transformation', *Economic Development and Cultural Change 34* (No. 2).

Leslie, J., M. Lycette and M. Buvinic (1986), *Weathering Economic Crises: The Crucial Role of Women in Health*. International Center for Research on Women, Washington, DC.

Lewenhak, S. (1988), *The Revaluation of Women's Work*, Croom Helm, London.

Lewis, J.P. and V. Kallab, eds. (1986), *Development Strategies Reconsidered.* Overseas Development Institute, London.

Lim, L. (1981), 'Women's Work in Multinational Electronics Factories', in R. Dambert and M. Cain (eds.), *Women and Technological Change in Developing Countries*, Boulder Press, Colorado.

Loxley, J. (1986), *Debt and Disorder: External Financing for Development*, Westview Press/North South Institute, Ottawa.

Mair, L., 'Women in the World – the Challenge of the Nineties', Paper presented at the University of South Dakota, April 1986.

Marei, Wafaa (1985). 'The Importance of Research and Training to the Integration of Women in Development', INSTRAW, Santo Domingo.

Moser, C. (1987), 'Impact of Recession and Structural Adjustment at the Micro-level: Low Income Women and their Households in Guayaquil, Ecuador. Part 1', UNICEF Regional Programme for Women in Development, Americas and Caribbean Regional Office, UNICEF Bogotá.

Mosley and Jolly (1987), 'Health Policy and Programme Options: Compensating for the Negative Effects of Economic Adjustment', *Adjustment with a Human Face*, UNICEF, Clarendon Press, Oxford.

Naylor, R.T. (1987), *Hot Money and the Politics of Debt*, Linden Press/Simon and Schuster, New York.

North-South Institute (1985). 'Women, and International Development Cooperation: Trade and Investment', INSTRAW, *Study on the Role of Women in International Economic Relations*, Santo Domingo.

North-South Roundtable on Money and Finance (1985), 'Statement of the Roundtable on Money and Finance, New York, 13–14 Dec. 1985', North-South Roundtable Publications, Pakistan.

Paguio B., 'No Bed of Roses for Filipinas Abroad', Depthnews Women's Feature

Service, Manila. ISIS/WICCE, March 1988.

Pala Okeyo, A. (1985), *Toward Strategies for Strengthening the Position of Women in Food Production: An Overview and Proposals on Africa*, INSTRAW, Dominican Republic.

Palmer, Ingrid (1988). 'Gender Issues in Structural Adjustment of Sub-Saharan Agriculture and some Demographic Implications', World Employment Programme Research Working Paper No. 166, ILO Geneva.

Pontifical Commission 'Iusticia et Pax', *At the Service of the Human Community: an Ethical Approach to the International Debt Question*, Vatican Press.

Potter, George Ann (1988), *Dialogue on Debt: Alternative Analyses and Solutions*, Center of Concern, 3700 13th Street NE, Washington DC.

Psacharopoulos, G., 'Education and Development: A Review', *The World Bank Research Observer*, Vol. 3 No. 1, January 1988.

Sahn, D.E., (1987) 'Changes in the living standards of the poor in Sri Lanka during a period of macroeconomic restructuring', *World Development*.

Sebstad, J. (1982), *Struggle and Development among Self-employed Women*, USAID, Washington DC.

Sen, G., and C. Grown (1985), *Development, Crisis and Alternative Visions: Third World Women's Perspective*. Development Alternatives with Women for a New Era (DAWN), New Delhi.

Stern, Brigitte. *The Changing Role of Women in International Economic Relations*. International Research and Training Institute for the Advancement of Women (INSTRAW), Dominican Republic.

Stewart, F. (1987), 'The Evolution of the Economic Crisis and its Impact on the Poor' an address to the UN/NGO Workshop held in Oxford, 1987; also: 'Supporting Productive Employment among Vulnerable Groups'; and 'Monitoring and Statistics for Adjustment with a Human Face', *Adjustment with a*

Human Face, UNICEF, Clarendon Press, Oxford.

United Nations (1981),'Women and the Establishment of a New Economic Order: A Selection of Recent Articles and Statements' (Mimeo), New York; *also:* (1985), 'Report of the World Conference to Review and Appraise the Achievements of the United Nations Decade for Women: Equality, Development and Peace, Nairobi 15–26 July 1985', New York; *also:* Report on UN Interregional Seminar on Women and the Economic Crisis: Impact, Policies and Prospects. UN/CSDHA Vienna, 28 October 1988; *see also:* 'Possible Social Consequences of the Economic Crisis: Increased violence in the family and in society', Working Paper prepared for the Interregional Seminar on Women and the Economic Crisis, Vienna, UNOV/CSDHA/DAW; *also:* 'The Debt Problem: Acute and Chronic Aspects', *UN Journal of Development Planning* No. 16, United Nations, New York, 1985; *also:* UNGA Resolution 41/202, 8 December 1986, on strengthening of economic cooperation to resolve external debt problems of developing countries, UN General Assembly, New York, 1986.

UNCTAD (1986). *Trade and Development Report 1986*, Chapter VI. United Nations Conference on Trade and Development, UN New York, 1986; *also:* 'The Final Act of UNCTAD VII'. Sections on Debt and Resources for Development and the Least Developed Countries, UN Conference on Trade and Development, Geneva, August 1987.

UNDP (1985). *The Debt Dilemma*, United Nations Development Programme, New York; *also:* 'UNDP Activities: Adjustment Measures and Policy Reforms', in *Programme Planning*, doc. DP/1987/27, New York, 22 April 1987.

UNDP and North-South Round Table (1986) 'Adjustment and Growth with Human Development' (The Salzburg Statement), UNDP-NSRT Meeting, 7–9

September 1986. UNDP-NSRT, New York.

UNICEF (1987), *The Invisible Adjustment: Poor Women and the Economic Crisis.* The Americas and The Caribbean Regional Office, Regional Programme on Women and Development, UNICEF Santiago; *also: Within Human Reach: A Future for Africa's Children*, UNICEF New York, 1985; *also: State of the World's Children 1987, 1988, 1989 and 1990.*

UNICEF/WFP (1986). *Food Aid and the Well-Being of Children in the Developing World*, UNICEF/World Food Programme, New York.

UNIFEM (1986), 'UNIFEM Experience of a Revolving Loan Fund', UN Development Fund for Women, Occasional Paper No. 4, United Nations, New York.

United Nations University/World Institute for Development Economics Research (1987), *Stabilisation Programmes in Developing Countries*, UNU/WIDER, Helsinki.

World Bank (1986), *Financing Adjustment with Growth in Sub-Saharan Africa, 1986–90*, Washington, DC; *also: Poverty and Hunger: Issues and Options for Food Security in Developing Countries*, World Bank, Washington DC; *also: Protecting the Poor during Periods of Adjustment*, Staff Paper prepared for April 1987 meeting of the Development Committee, World Bank, Washington, DC. *also:* 'Barriers to Adjustment and Growth in the World Economy', in *World Development Report 1987*, Oxford University Press, New York.

World Commission on Environment and Development (1987), 'The Role of the International Economy', in *Our Common Future*. Oxford University Press.

World Employment Programme (International Labour Office), 'The Crisis in the North and the South: The Impact of the World Recession on Employment and Poverty', in *Basic Needs and Employment*, WEP Working Paper No. 59, ILO Geneva, June 1985; *also:* Jamal, Vali. 'Structural Adjustment and Food Security in Uganda', WEP Working Paper No. 73, ILO Geneva, 1985; *also:* Tabatabai, Hamid, 'Economic Decline, Access to Food and Structural Adjustment in Ghana', WEP Working Paper No. 80, ILO Geneva, 1986; *also:* 'Stabilisation, Adjustment and Poverty', International Employment Policies, WEP Working Paper No. 1, ILO Geneva, January 1986. In the same series: Ubogu, R.E. and Umo, J.U., 'Impacts of the External Sector on Employment and Equity: The Case of Brazil and Chile', WEP Working Paper No. 6, 1986; Cortazar, René 'Employment, Real Wages and External Constraint: The case of Brazil and Chile', WEP Working Paper No. 8, October 1986; Mertens, L. 'Employment and Stabilisation in Mexico', WEP Working Paper No. 10. December 1986; Van der Hoeven, R. and Vandemoortele, J., 'Kenya: Stabilisation and Adjustment Experiences (1979–1984) and Prospects for Future Development', WEP Working Paper No. 11, January 1987; Ndulo, Manenga and Sakala, Martin. 'Stabilisation Policies in Zambia: 1976–1985', WEP Working Paper No. 13, 1987; *also: World Recession and Global Interdependence: Effects on Employment, Poverty and Policy Formation in Developing Countries*, World Employment Programme, ILO Geneva 1987.

World Food Council (1987), 'The Global State of Hunger and Malnutrition and the Impact of Economic Adjustment on Food and Hunger Problems'. Doc. WFC/1987/2, WFC Rome 8 April 1987.

World Food Programme (1985), 'Evaluation of Food Aid for Price Stabilisation and Emergency Food Reserve Projects: A Study of WFP-assisted projects in Tanzania, Botswana, Mauritania, Niger and Mali in 1984', Occasional Paper No. 2, WFP Rome, September 1985; *also:* 'Roles of Food Aid in Structural and Sectoral Adjustment', doc. WFP/CFA 23/5 Add. 1, WFP Rome, 3 April 1987; *also:*

'Food Aid Strategy for Women in
Development', doc. WFP/CFA 23/7, WFP
Rome, 17 March 1987.

World Health Organisation (1987), *Economic
Support for National Health for All
Strategies*. Selected Bibliography. Doc.
WHO/HSC/87.2; *also:* 'Executive Summary
and Key Issues', Fortieth World health
Assembly, doc. A.40/Technical
Discussions/1; Background document
A.40/Technical Discussions/2; and 'Report
of the Technical Discussions on
"Economic Support for National Health
for All Strategies"' doc. A/40/Technical
Discussions/4, WHO Geneva, May
1987.

INDEX